BOOKENDS

A Partial History of the Book Trade in Brighton

JOHN SHIRE

To Pete
Thanks
from
John

Invocations Press

...stuff'd with volumes from bottom to top ...the last link in that long chain ...no-one ever thought he was gay ...looking after hippy booksellers ...an arsenal of explosives ...that little dash of colour and sanity ...actually a freak accident ...of apoplectic proportions ...a troglodyte's existence ...we've got paper bombs ...shouting at customers ...complete stranger ...last Dickensian ...too dim to live on social security...not just a bookshop... death by cheese sandwich...

BOOKENDS

A Partial History of the Book Trade in Brighton

© John Shire 2011

j.shire@virgin.net.

Visit the BOOKENDS facebook page for discussions, pictures and more information.
www.libraryofthesphinx.co.uk
www.flickr.com/photos/johnshire
Published by Invocations Press.

Pictures, collages and advertisements from *Yellow Pages*, the *Brighton Voice*, *Brighton Head & Freak Mag*, the *Punter*, Brighton History Centre, Grimoire catalogue, Rare Books & Special Collections at the Jubilee Library.

Design and photography by John Shire
Cover: Losing Roman Marbles.
Back Cover: Out the Back at Colin Page.

ISBN: 978 0 9568021 0 1

What a history of human excesses a second-hand bookshop is! ...Every revolution is a reaction, every leap-forward a renaissance, every new thought a returning to a spring that has been choked up. Second-hand bookshops are the oases where these old fountains of living water can still flow.

-John Cowper Powys

*There's more to life than books you know,
But not much more, not much more.*

-Morrissey

CONTENTS

TO CAPTURE A STRANGE CITY — 1
The End of Books

BRIGHTON — 7
Beginning at the End of the Line,
without Crush or Confusion

LIKE EVERYONE ELSE — 26
Masons and Suicides

THE FILTH — 35
Bill Butler and the Unicorn Bookshop

THIEVES AND POETS — 59
Symposium and Solstice

THE ESSENTIAL HERESIES — 70
The 70's and the Public House Bookshop

A ROARING BARGAIN — 82
The Odd Volume, Tall Storeys and Picture Books

GIN AND ASHES — 88
Bredons, Beals and Combridges

OCCULT POWERS — 96
    Trafalgar Street and its Skulls

CHAOS AND OLD NIGHT — 105
    N F Brookes

PAST HISTORIC — 112
    Holleyman and Treacher

THE HEART OF THINGS — 120
    Ben Hutchinson, Colin Page and John Loska

BRIGHTON: A SURVEY — 126

APOCRYPHA — 136

BIBLIOPOLYGRAPHY — 141
    A Neologism of Brighton Bookshops

BIBLIOGRAPHY — 147

RANDOM MISCELLANEOUS COMPANY — 152
    Acknowledgements

INDEX — 155

The Bookſeller, 1.
ſelleth Books
in a Bookſellers Shop, 2.
of which he writeth
a Catalogue, 3.
The Books are placed
on Shelves, 4.
and are laid open for uſe
upon a Deſk, 5.
A Multitude of Books
is called a Library, 6.

TO CAPTURE A STRANGE CITY – The End of Books

>Collectors are people with a tactical instinct; their experience teaches them that when they capture a strange city, the smallest antique shop can be a fortress, the most remote stationery store a key position. How many cities have revealed themselves to me in the marches I undertook in the pursuit of books!
>   - Walter Benjamin

In 2002, number 12 Queen's Road, a black and green relic, gave up its books for the last time.

Now yet another small café, this tall thin building remained undecorated for years, overshadowed by the constantly changing name and décor of the pub next door. It had been the original bookshop of the legendary N.F. Brookes but the place had been closed for many months and, as far as I could tell, only used as storage for the larger and more recently-closed two unit shop on the other side of the road. Now, however, a few people were going in and out, armed to the teeth, possibly even the back teeth, with books. Intrigued, I crossed the road to investigate.

"I can't bear destroying books," said the man charged with clearing up the place for new occupiers, "So help yourself. Honestly, take what you want."

The first part goes without saying: who would consciously align themselves with the book-burners of this world after all? The second is a magical, almost unimaginable, sentiment for a bibliophile to hear. Naturally, I had been in here before. The original Brookes shop was of the traditional kind: uninviting to most and deliberately challenging to a few. By that I mean that it presented a surface of chaos and a tantalising depth of incalculable value. At least that's what you hoped. At the rear of the front room, narrow stairs led to two upper floors packed with books. Initially at least, and certainly to the uninitiated, the books were unconscionably confused. But that doesn't matter. Find the one that catches your eye and then move on, bouncing around like some short-lived sub-atomic particle, fetched up for a few fleeting moments in a massive cloud chamber. Of course you always knew that there was a secret order to be found if you simply knew how to look. Or the occult remnants of what had once been order.

Now though, without an owner and undoubtedly marked for redevelopment, things had taken on a despairing aspect. Besides a few other opportunist vultures like me, the shop was largely empty. What was left was twisted and water-damaged, the books on jerry-built shelves, falling over themselves with no support from companions. Looking out of the small windows on the back stairs, I remember seeing cramped ancient outhouses, possibly medieval in origin, full to the ceiling with boxes of repeated titles, remainders bought for a pittance at auction and becoming increasingly unsaleable with each passing year. These still remained, I noticed. Not even the hardiest would dare venture into those nether regions. Probably the back door wouldn't open. I imagined grim philistines shovelling this literary waste into a skip.

The basement was the worst. Down there, even before the closure, awful things had surely been left to fester. Stepping off the stairs into the gloom there was no sign of a floor. Instead books and papers up to three feet thick provided a dank carpet of mossy, unread words. It was miserable. But we soldiered on regardless, scavenging, looking for that unnoticed diamond in the mud. I found half a complete bibliography of Hermann Hesse, an eighteenth-century leather-bound history of Greek tyrants, several copies of the memoir *Queens* by 'Pickles', a local gay celebrity from the eighties, then, separately and on different days, a complete two-part monograph on the archaeological excavations of Easter Island, a series of Maggs Brothers (London antiquarian book dealers) catalogues of Incunabula from the 1930's, a modern history of Western Architecture and a book that is, in 2009, exactly one hundred years old. It is the *History of Ibn Miskawayh* in the E.J.W. Gibb Memorial series, volume VII, No. I. It is a facsimile edition. It is in Arabic script.

I cannot read Arabic. The preface (by the Principe di Teano) tells me what period the history covers and something about the author but, still, I cannot read Arabic.

It doesn't matter. That's what second-hand bookshops do for you. If you don't understand that, then I'm afraid you've picked up the wrong book. Casual visitors can be dismayed and disconcerted by the disorder and complexity of the majority of second-hand bookshops, so it is perfectly understandable why they are not everyone's cup of tea. And it is rare that attitudes and presentation conform to modern notions of customer service. One can need guts and determination to successfully negotiate certain establishments. That, for some, is all part of the fun, the thrill of the chase, more "hawks and vultures" than browsing sheep[1]. Those who work in bookshops, as George Orwell did for a time, can generally give as good as they get, too.

---

[1] (Cowper Powys, The Pleasures of Literature, 1938)

> First edition snobs were much commoner than lovers of literature, but oriental students haggling over cheap textbooks were commoner still, and vague-minded women looking for birthday presents for their nephews were commonest of all.[1]

> But the bookseller's shop, I must tell all about it,
> The place would be dull as a dunghill without it.
>
> — Mr G.S. Carey in *The Tagg or Brighthelmstone Guide* 1777

How books and booksellers are welcomed and supported by local inhabitants can say a great deal about a town. The books of Brighton have a significant but awkward history in this respect, with embarrassments and achievements in equal measure. In his younger days during the late nineteenth century, the novelist John Cowper Powys stayed in and around the town, long before he began to write his monumental West Country novels. His memoirs provide invaluable information about the retailers of his time. To put it mildly, his passion for bookshops was quite intense:

> But one thing is certain. Though books, as Milton says, may be the embalming of mighty spirits, they are also the resurrection of rebellious, reactionary, fantastical and wicked spirits! In books dwell all the demons and all the angels of the human mind. It is for this reason that a bookshop – especially a second-hand bookshop – is an arsenal of explosives, an armoury of revolutions, an opium-den of reactions...

---

[1] (Orwell, 1936)

> In a second-hand bookshop are the horns of the altar where all the outlawed thoughts of humanity can take refuge! Here, like desperate bandits, hide all the reckless progeny of our wild, dark, self-lacerating hearts. A bookshop is a powder-magazine, a dynamite-shed, a drug-store of poisons, a bar of intoxicants, a den of opiates, an island of Sirens.
>
> — Cowper Powys - *The Pleasures of Literature*
> 1938

These days I doubt many people would make the connection between his gushing, poetical suggestions of sex, drugs and revolutionary terrorism and any kind of bookshop they are likely to have encountered. But you've got to love that kind of wild potential. If only they were really that interesting...

In the face of e-books, i-pads, short attention spans, face-book, dwindling resources and never enough room or time, books are under increasing pressure from all directions. Their life cycle is not what it was. A glance around Waterstone's or a supermarket will tell you that there are more books born now than ever before. But they are also more likely to lead short and, on the whole, unrewarding lives. Many are now delivered directly onto the internet as instant ghosts, cutting out that old-fashioned middle stage of corporeality. Immortality is cheap now and what does it profit a man, to gain the whole world and lose his soul? But this doesn't matter; books are just things, tools to be used up and discarded. Aren't they? Am I asking too many rhetorical questions?

Books used to go from publication to bookshops to bookshelves to second-hand status and back to bookshelves, disappearing into dusty oblivion at odd moments en route. With the rise of internet selling and the subsequent loss of many actual second-hand bookshops, books may well ride this merry-go-round for longer than ever. But once again, there are so many - too many - and they will end up pulped and skipped, ignored and unloved. The extremes are here.

So on the cusp of what may be yet another publishing revolution, another painful evolution in the presentation of the printed word; here is a book about one small city, its bookshops and their inhabitants.

BRIGHTON – Beginning at the End of the Line, without Crush or Confusion

In the early 1990's Brighton still clung to a decent array of bookshops. While an antiquarian few might prefer to look further back at the hey-day of George Sexton's outlets with delight, it was Duke Street that boasted the established giants of Colin Page and Holleyman & Treacher then. Even Leon Morelli's London-based Pharos Group opened a branch of Quinto's bookshop, in an act of expansive folly, right next door to Colin Page in 1986. It didn't last. Inland, under the station bridge and in the as-yet-unreconstructed area of the North Laines, Trafalgar Street was home to the record and bookshop Wax Factor, the occult specialist Adam Ball and the Trafalgar Bookshop. Over to the east, Courthouse Steps Books, Tall Storeys, Brimstones and the Studio Bookshop continued toward Kemp Town Books, while on the route from the station to the sea and unmissable to all beach-orientated tourists arriving by train, N.F. Brookes' groaning windows consistently amazed and amused passers-by.

"The books are in Brighton and Brighton is in the books"; The collages that illustrate Clark Ashton Smith's *A Rendezvous in Averoigne*[1] feature cut-up bits of the Brighton Pavilion, a minor fact probably lost on a great many people but auspiciously obvious to my friend Mike and I as we strolled happily away from Tall Storeys at some time in the mid-nineties. He had brought the book from London to augment my increasingly repetitive collection of Lovecraftiana[2] (how many copies of the story 'At the Mountains of Madness'[3] does one man need, after all? Not nine, I'll wager). Fortified by the requisite, if unfeasibly large, fried breakfast, we trawled the bookshops as usual.

In St. James Street on the way to Kemp Town, Tall Storeys was accurately named. A thin building with four floors whose stock became increasingly interesting during the ascent of the tiny stairs that wound their way up the back of the shop. But that wasn't all. On that fateful day we discovered the wonders of the secret top storey, the locked room at the end of the stairs. On receipt of the key, and with our bags as collateral, we entered this hallowed realm with trepidation.

Thankfully this was to be one of those times when Lovecraft's dead gods were looking favourably upon us. Among the selection of modern firsts were several more Arkham House editions (the same publisher as my new Clark Ashton Smith), some of them first editions from the forties. With a little help from Mike, though we were both outrageously poor at the time, I spent £95 on two books. Others that I would happily have purchased then and there, slipped away before we could return with sufficient funds. Still, the books are in Brighton.

---

[1] Arkham House, 1988, illustrations by Jeffrey K. Potter
[2] Any items related to the early 20th Century American horror writer, H.P.Lovecraft. I seem to be congenitally unable to avoid the man and have been reliably informed that, when enormously drunk, I am given to claiming that almost everything comes back to, and possibly even revolves around, this short-lived and very dead American writer.
[3] Soon to be a major film, as the saying goes.

Happy days. Good times. If you like that sort of thing. And Brighton has always swung that way.

Brighton owes its first lease of life to a book. In 1750 the Oxford University Press published *De Tabe Glandulari: Sive Usu Aquae Marinae in Morbis Glandularum Dissertatio* (Glandular Diseases: or a Dissertation on the Use of Sea-Water in Affections of the Glands). Not, you might think, the most riveting read. By 1753 the English version was popular with the medical profession and, despite a distinctly unpromising title to contemporary eyes, the book became the motive for the first wave of visitations to Brighton. The author, Dr Richard Russell, practised in Lewes and, though he did not mention Brighton by name, certainly implied that the town's position was ideal for his sea-water bathing treatments.

With the increase in unhealthy visitors looking for salty cures for their ailments, Brighton grew apace, providing the first major wave of hotels and boarding houses for all walks of society. And, like many other suddenly fashionable towns of the eighteenth century, Brighton boasted a large number of circulating libraries, too (it was the books that did the circulating, not the libraries themselves).

Forerunners of the modern public library, subscription and circulating libraries, though similar in many important respects, arose from separate backgrounds and favoured different clientele. Subscription libraries tended to be more expensive to join, more exclusive and attracted that particular class of eighteenth-century gentleman interested in theology, biography, history and the sciences; the class of men who, at the very least, enjoyed the appearance of dabbling in academia. The success of circulating libraries, on the other hand, was paralleled by the rise of the novel and supported by women as both readers and writers. It should come as no surprise that Brighton favoured the latter over the former.

From 1760 to the beginning of the nineteenth century there were around sixteen booksellers in Brighton. At least nine of these also ran circulating libraries. Three were originally centred on the Steine (or Steyne, as it was then), the first being set up in 1760 by a Mr Baker, bookseller of Tunbridge Wells. The library itself, a single-storey timber building with an arched verandah, was the first building on the eastern side of the Steine (around the beginning of St. James Street now), which meant visitors had to cross the marshy, occasional course of the Wellesbourne stream or walk round the stagnant pool that overflowed into Pool Valley to get there: all of which is a far cry from the glass ecology of the current Jubilee Library. Fishermen would still drag their boats up onto the Steine for safety in winter and during bad weather. Beside Baker's library was a raised section of ground that served as a bandstand.

> On [the Steyne] is a fmall, but neat orcheftra, in which a felect band performs twice a day, during the feafon. Here, likewife are fome fhops, and the circulating library, which is stocked with a good collection of books, of which the company have the ufe for the feafon, on fubfcribing what they think proper.[1]

The most important book in these libraries was the register. Any person of consequence would sign in at the beginning of their visit and then casually peruse the other signatures to check on whom else, eligible, notorious or related, was in town for the entertainments. The early libraries became extraordinarily popular as places to gather and gossip, to exchange information and to be entertained or entertaining. It is possible that sometimes even a little reading went on.

Baker's was taken over by a Miss Widget, then Mr Thomas in 1779. Then Mr Dudlow, followed by Mr Gregory, then Mr Donaldson and, finally, Thomas Lucombe. When Gregory's was taken over by Donaldson's one name was simply written over another on the stamps inserted into their books.

---

[1] (unknown, The Brighthelmstone Directory &c. &c., 1769). Brighton is famous for "fome fhops" after all.

Rivals soon began to appear, like Mr Bowen's establishment, closer to the centre of town. The author Fanny Burney was once a visitor here and mentioned the experience in her diaries. A third library, where "the dice are often rattled to some tune, and bank-notes transferred from one hand to another with as little ceremony as...a quack doctor's draughts to their patients"[1] was established by Mr Donaldson Jnr, taken over by Mr Osborne and finally run by Mr Nathaniel Turner. A favourite spot, due to  a fine view, was Messrs Donaldson and Wilkes emporium at Marine Parade (afterwards Mr Pollard, then Messrs Tuppen and Walker).

It is some indication of the popularity and significance of these social hotspots that so many changed hands in such a small area over a period of less than a hundred years. They all provided somewhere for a summer visitor at the Regency town to sit and chat, perhaps after an invigorating stroll around the town while arguing the architectural merits of the Prince of Wales' new residence on the Steyne (which, while certainly expensive, was not yet the elaborate oriental fantasia it later became. Visitors didn't like it even before the indulgent new designs: it was "gaudy but not gay"[2]. Things may be different now).

John Byng, 5th Viscount Torrington and noted diarist, was not impressed by his first encounter with Brighton in 1788 either:

---

[1] (Erredge, 1862)
[2] (Underwood, 1978)

> Brighton appeared in a fashionable unhappy Bustle, with such a harpy Set of painted Harlots as to appear to me as bad as Bond Street, in the Spring, at 3 o'clock, p.m...The Castle is reckoned a good Tavern, and so we found it completely; and most comfortably too, after out Walking the Steyne, entering the Booksellers Shops, sitting by the Sea Side and endeavouring to look like Old Residents...

Despite his evident distaste for some of the locals, the eminent gentleman reserves a good word or two for the views and the bookshops, selecting a description, cut from a contemporary guidebook, of Crawford's Library to include in his notes:

> Crawford's library commands a delightful view of the Downs, on the north side of the town, and also a very pleasing prospect of the Sea, the Cliff, which rises here to a considerable height, and many other objects, which even separately considered, yield much satisfaction, but the whole grouped in so pleasing a variety, gives to the face of nature an appearance, than which nothing more beautifully picturesque can possibly be imagined; and being fitted up in a commodious manner, and entirely sheltered from the sun, it is esteemed a polite and agreeable rendezvous; where, when conversation fails to prove sufficiently interesting, recourse may be had to books suited to every taste.

That is the advertising spin, the promotional material. And even there, books are mentioned only as a last resort. What went on and what people thought of the libraries was not so simple.

This is still the case even now. The Jubilee Library doesn't have enough decent books. But it should have a café (because there aren't enough of those in Brighton...). There is too great a focus on multi-media preoccupations, interactive involvements; the kids are too noisy. Bookshops have too many concessions in them. There is too much or too little internet access. How dare you not have Wi-fi!

These are contemporary concerns but not new arguments. The circulating libraries of the late eighteenth century had similar issues. They were never that fantasy of quiet contemplation and perfect literary accessibility. Once upon a time, perhaps in the late nineteenth century, perhaps somewhere in, say, London, there was that archetypal library moment from which all others digress: the room (private or public?) was quiet and warm and everything was within reach. There was no need to write any more, barely any need to read. All had been achieved. Everything before and since is a long way from that. The degradation of books has a long and illustrious history.

Sometimes people were barely concerned about the books at all. And, like Viscount Torrington, the very openness of the Circulating libraries did not always suit a visitor's taste.

> To the sound of this musick I march'd to a shop,
> I saw stuff'd with volumes from bottom to top;
> Where books of all languages, and of all sizes,
> Were set up in lots, - and deliver'd as prizes
> To him, who could best shake his elbow at dice,
> Not him who best read or expounded them nice.[1]

> I write now from Bowen's shop, where he has been settled about three days I think. And here comes in one man hopping, and asks for Russell on Sea-water; another tripping, and begs to have the last new novel sent him home tonight; one lady tumbles the ballads about

---

[1] Poem from *New Brighthelmstone Directory*, 1770 in (Smith, 2002).

and fingers the harpsichord, which stands here at every blockheads mercy; and another looks over the Lilliputian library, and purchases Polly Sugarcake for her long-legged missy.

- Letter from Mrs Thrale in Brighton to Miss Fanny Burney, 14th July 1780

I was yawning at Bowen's over the first volume of *Cecilia*, when in came a Lady whistling a cotillion and flanking her whip against her petticoat: she wore a purple Habit lined with pink silk and a Hat which recalled to mind the rich Tiara of the great Tom Thumb. 'The Town was very full, she said, but the weather very unfavourable: the Duchess had been confined to her room with a fever ever since she had been there' – and then looking at the raffles, but succumbing to none, tossing into confusion a whole counter of Books, and asking the price of all without purchasing any – and calling Shergold a foolish fellow for having a *Dress* Ball in the Evening, tho she knew he could not help it – turned swiftly round on one peg-heel and wisked out of the shop with a "tol-de-rol, tum tum"!
Such are the light liberties which Women are permitted and chose to take...

- Anthony Highmore
A Ramble on the Coast of Sussex, 1782

Donaldson's and Walker's Libraries, the former at the angle of St. James's St. east of the Steyne, the latter on the Marine Parade, are fashionable and amusive lounges when the town is full. The principal occupations of their frequenters are, engaging in the raffles for various trinkets, articles of Tunbridge ware, &c., sold by the proprietors; listening to music, both vocal and instrumental, provided for the entertainment of the company; or pacing backwards and forwards, simply to 'see and be seen', for a whole evening perhaps, from one of these places of universal resort to another.

- Thomas Cromwell
Excursions in the County of Sussex, 1822

Ladies with whips, men tripping, music by blockheads? Sounds like Brighton already. Books and reading barely get a mention or are casually dismissed with an airy wave of the hand. Raffles based in the libraries were so popular that they were eventually made illegal, only to be replaced by 'Trinket Auctions', which amounted to the same thing. Then the card game of Loo, or Pam (after the Knave of Clubs), was played in the evenings, with blinds pulled down over the bookshelves and the windows.

In spite of this, by the first half of the nineteenth century, books really were the thing. For those fifty years, one hundred and three booksellers graced the streets of Brighton. They lived and died, rented new premises, handed on the trade to sons or daughters and went bankrupt, but not necessarily in that order. Again, twenty-nine of them ran circulating libraries, clustering on the eastern side of the town, some down North Street, more along St. James Street and prestigious ones around Marine Parade and the Esplanade with views of the great grey English Channel. Many of them conducted related trades from what must have been rather elaborate premises: print selling, bookbinding, newspaper publishing, engraving, etching; there were stationers, quill makers, sealing wax manufacturers and some, like Crawford's, provided postal services. Others, perhaps less wedded to the purity of the written word, also ran pharmacies, jewellers, insurance agencies, toyshops and hardware stores from the bookshop premises. One was even a coal merchant as well, which doesn't bode well for the condition of the books.

Apart from St. James Street, booksellers tended to huddle together in a town as small but perfectly formed as Brighton appeared then. Between them, North Street, East Street, Ship Street and Meeting House Lane saw twenty-nine booksellers come and go. They fought for custom with grandiose titles: Joseph Cordwell's "Repository of Arts", Mr Choat's "Emporium of Literature" and Thomas Lucombe's "Royal Library and Literary Saloon". Choat's in particular was very well established (and also referred to itself as a Royal Library) having been in existence since at least 1806. It provides the back drop to a painting by G.M. Brighty of a bookseller at the Emporium, Richard Gregory, not directly named but referred to as 'A Well-Known Character at Brighton'. Colin Page, another well-known bookseller in Brighton, has a print of this on the wall of his own library.

Choat's became Loder's and eventually ended up in the hands of Robert Folthorp, one of these grand gentlemen of literature and a successful survivor into the latter half of the century. He ran yet another Royal Library, at 170 North Street. His *Court Guide and General Directory for Brighton* lists a total of 53 booksellers and stationers around the town in 1856. Folthorp's advertisement for themselves in their own Guide of that year shows a special concern for the younger generation: "Library for the Young - A choice Collection of Books, more especially adapted for the Entertainment and Instruction of Juvenile Readers, has been recently added; and great care has been taken to exclude all publications of an immoral or doubtful tendency." Don't forget this. Brighton, while outwardly keen on doubtful tendencies of late, also has a habit of exclusion.

These early booksellers' names are now long forgotten and impossible to separate from the circulating libraries – Dollman's in Western Road, Burrett's of Waterloo Street, Hove, Style's in North Street, Sugg's of St. James Street and Grant's Library and Reading Room in Castle Square.

The history of Grant's establishment provides a series of exemplary illustrations of the position of booksellers in the early 19th century. Orphaned at the age of nine in 1827, William Grant was taken in by John Jones and his wife. When Jones died, Grant took over his premises in Castle Square, changing them from a declining coach office business to become Brighton's first newsagent. Only a year later, in 1839, Grant was in Lewes prison for a libel against Charles Andrews, another bookseller in St. James Street. As the law stood then, Grant was guilty of libel simply by selling publications containing libellous articles (in this case the Paul Pry magazine): a remarkable position to find oneself in from today's perspective. And he was not alone. Several other agents sold this publication and were similarly brought to court. It seems obvious now that this was all rather untenable and even Andrews, who was, after all, a bookseller himself and not exempt from such arcane legal logic, chose to recommend extreme leniency. Grant was given a conditional discharge and a fine of £20.

After this unpleasantness the business expanded to 72 Queen's Road, next to the station. "Grant's News Office" boasted the latest leading newspapers from around the world and there were over 10,000 books in the circulating library to be read, purchased or loaned. Success, however, came and went again. As a result of financial losses in the mid-1850's, combined with increasing competition, Grant went bankrupt. He continued to run the Castle Square business until his death in 1860 when his daughter Elizabeth and later her husband, Bartholomew Parker Bidder, took it over until 1863 when they too finally lost out to bankruptcy. Defeated, they moved to London.[1]

Eventually though, "...the literary character of which the Steine formerly boasted [was] now entirely gone."[2] As the nineteenth century wore on, private ownership came to outweigh

---

[1] Andy Grant, a descendant of William's and a Brighton historian, kindly provided this story.
[2] (Erredge, 1862)

public enlightenment and books were bought and owned rather than circulated and discussed (or ignored). Toward the turn of the century, and judging by the slightly arbitrary listings in town guides, things still looked pretty healthy. Towner's Brighton Directory of 1897 lists 107 Booksellers, Stationers and Newsvendors, though these divisions are not necessarily helpful as this is much the same as including all current newsagents in a listing of bookshops today. Of the 107, four booksellers are intriguingly described as *fancy*, one as a wholesaler and only two are specified as *second-hand*[1].

> Books of interest to the collector are rarely met with in the lanes, there being close by in North Street and Ship Street respectively two great warehouses for the sale of books, new and old.[2]

During his 1896 sojourn in Southwick, John Cowper Powys (author of *Weymouth Sands* and *A Glastonbury romance*, to name only two of his enormous novels) discovered the poems of W. B. Yeats in North's Bookshop "...on what I think was called the Western Road..." The vagaries of both memory and Brighton's roads probably mean that this is E. North of 30 Church Road, Hove: "I can even recall the figure of Mr. North himself...a lean, reserved little man with a coal-black beard." Powys also remembers "an amazing second-hand shop...in the very heart of Brighton, within a few hundred yards of the Regent's famous pavilion. It was kept by a dignified little man called 'Mr Smith' whose chief assistant was a huge, black-bearded fellow, resembling the ogres in fairy-tales but with one of the mildest and most Early-Christian countenances I have ever seen." A William Joshua Smith is a likely candidate here –"Bookseller, Libraries Purchased"- at 41, 42 and 43 North Street from 1864

---

[1] James Thorpe at 53 Ship Street, later taken over by George Sexton, and Alf Keeping at 9 Meeting House Lane.
[2] (Sala, 1895) Presumably Treachers and James Thorpe's or W.J. Smith's.

until his death in 1911.[1] Smith had bought a book business from Charles Hindley who started selling books from 10 Meeting House Lane way back in 1845. Smith then expanded to 105 St. James Street in 1855 and finally to the North Street premises in 1859. The industrious Smith compiled scrapbooks of articles and illustrations of local interest, now known as 'Smith's Cuttings', which have become an invaluable historical resource. They are held in the Brighton History Centre. In 1884 Mr Smith also published this gem of a book: *The Genuine History of the Inhuman and Unparalleled Murders of Mr William Galley, a custom-house officer and Mr Daniel Chater, a shoe-maker, by fourteen notorious smugglers with the trials and execution of seven of the criminals at Chichester 1748-49, illustrated with Seven Plates, Description of the Barbarous Cruelties*. Snappy titles had yet to become an effective marketing tool. Violence and gore still did the trick though.

Cowper Powys is a veritable mine of description when it comes to Brighton bookshops. Unfortunately he doesn't name names. But then again, he appears to have spent most of the late 1890s at Southwick, and later outside Lewes, going slightly mad while eyeing up young women on the beach and looking for expensive pornography. So perhaps a little artistic circumspection was in order.

---

[1] (Beever)

There was [yet] another second-hand bookshop in those days, not far from the back alley retreat where I learnt – or should have learnt – that bedrooms hired at eighteen pence "for a short time" had a sedative rather than a provocative effect upon my amorous propensities. Here – in the bookshop I mean – there used to sit upon a high stool, which always made me think of the seat of Eli the Prophet used, a sort of venerable image of a book-collector, of apoplectic proportions, and with a heavy hydrocephalic head. The type of books *he* kept were both more expensive and more recondite than those in the "Smith" shop. They were indeed totally beyond my book knowledge. But the white-faced idol on the high stool was an incorrigible controversialist and full of the most erudite heresies. Argument he placed above cash; and with him I would argue by the hour upon the "Baconian Theory" [that Francis Bacon had written some or all of Shakespeare's plays], he defending it, I attacking it; till one day in the heat of discussion I roundly warned my gentleman that persons who "moved the bones", even in a spiritual sense, of the Man of Stratford, were in danger of falling under the curse of that great known Unknown. My heated words, as chance would have it, were grimly fulfilled; for, a few days after this particular argument, on reaching my friend's shop I found the shutters closed, and a little card affixed to the entrance announcing *the death of the proprietor.* [1]

---

[1] (Cowper Powys, Autobiography, 1934) Alf Keeping, of singularly un-bookish name, kept a second-hand bookshop at 9 Meeting House Lane in 1897. In 1898

Powys bought the risqué *Memoirs of Casanova* in French from here before discovering, in Eastbourne, and obviously to his great delight, a bookseller as young as himself who "...dealt in a sort of private lending library of fantastical "erotica"...This young man...gave me the impression of being a priest – a somewhat ambiguous young Ion – of the worship of the mother of Eros." It is heartening to note that Brighton's reputation for dodgy literary sleaze was well-established even by the turn of the century. Cowper Powys' association of books, bookshops, dubious sexual encounters, religious imagery and argument is an important counterpoint to the late-Victorian moralising evident in other literary establishments of the time. It also sounds an early-warning alarm for later controversial encounters between Brighton and its books.

And still, even before this, Charles Hindley, the precursor of William Joshua Smith at North Street, was not innocent of a little controversy either. Born in Clerkenwell in 1821, he became a bookseller and publisher in both London and Brighton but has since found some recognition as an early collector of urban folklore, publishing *Curiosities of Street Literature* in 1871. However, his more dubious claim to fame is his reprint of a small chap-book of the prophecies of the sixteenth-century Yorkshire witch known as Mother Shipton. This contains the exceptionally specific couplet informing readers that "The world to an end shall come, in eighteen hundred and eighty one". Rarely are prophecies so clear, mundane and worrying. Religious types of an apocalyptic bent took this kind of thing very seriously indeed. However, the earliest known version of Mother Shipton's utterances (in the British Library) contains no such lines. In the *Notes & Queries* journal of the 26th April, 1873, all was eventually revealed.

> Mr Charles Hindley, of Brighton, in a letter to
> us, has made a clean breast of having

---

it was run by the Goddard Brothers, then J.R.Hitchings in 1899 until 1908. It could have been any one of these men. Or someone else entirely.

fabricated the Prophecy quoted at page 450 of our last volume, with some ten others included in his reprint of a chap-book version, published in 1862.

Hindley also published the three volume *Old Book Collector's Miscellany* in 1871. Here there are tales of Dragons near Lewes, Siamese twins and Sir Gregory Nonsence and 'His Newes from no place' along with some obscure and frankly awful poetry. Hindley presented a copy to the Brighton Free Library on 12th August 1872 while living at 7b Rose Hill Terrace. They are now to be found in the Tony Miller Reading Room in the Jubilee Library. Hindley died in 1893, twelve years after the world was supposed to end.

Meanwhile, the larger subscription libraries developed, or began to devolve, into more general shops; places of retail where stationery and art materials (for the ladies, of course) could also be bought. Treachers in North Street was one of these, not simply dealing in books but providing a variety of related services such as book binding, map printing and assistance in general publishing ventures. They also acted as agents for two Insurance companies.

Two brothers from High Wycombe in Buckinghamshire established the business in the middle of the century. Harry and Charles Treacher had a prime spot: H. & C. Treachers occupied the prestigious corner of North Street and East Street, leasing the store from the Hanningtons family since 1845. The shop, managed by a Mr Clifford, had a bookseller's apprentice by the name of Edward Verrall Lucas who went on to become a famous authority on Charles Lamb, as well as a noted essayist, novelist and travel writer. His novel *Over Bemerton's* is the light but engaging tale of a man living above a bookshop in London. Whether he draws on his own experiences and real characters from Treacher's in the story is difficult to judge but he, and his main character, are far too diffident and polite to tell any exciting or contentious tales. The novel does include a gentle but almost obligatory dig at awkward customers though.

H. & C. Treacher's shop front was eventually rebuilt in 1924 to accommodate the new Hanningtons Department Store[1] and only the Treacher name survived into the 1990s as part of Holleyman & Treacher in Duke Street. There are many odd and obscure claims to fame in the book trade. One of Treacher's was their publication, in 1862, of the world's first illustrated stamp catalogue. *The Stamp Collectors Guide* by William Booty contained 200 facsimiles of stamps, drawn and lithographed by the author.

D. B. Friend and Co. "Booksellers, Stationers and Librarians" of 77 Western Road and 56 Church Road in Hove was another wide-ranging emporium. From 1867 this grand company began publishing a Brighton and Hove Almanack, like Folthorp before them, equally packed with all the who's and where's a visitor could possibly need and also with any number of their own advertisements, showing off the variety and quality of their services and products. They were certainly not shy about selling themselves. Apparently...

> It is generally admitted that their selection of *New Books*, in every department of Literature, is the largest and best selected in the South of England, the interior arrangement of 77 Western Road, Brighton, and of the West End Branch, at 56 Church Road, Hove, being of such a character as to make the same a Literary and Artistic Salon, where patrons may have the opportunity of inspecting the extensive stock without crush or confusion.
>
> Books which have gone out of print, and other scarce volumes, are inquired for without any expense to customers for advertising, &c.

---

[1] During its long reign as Brighton's premier Department store, Hannington's did host yet another bookshop: a branch of the Hatchard's chain.

> A very large and choice selection of handsomely bound volumes for school prizes, &c., prepared expressly for presentation.
> D. B. FRIEND & CO. have also a large stock of Stationery of every description, samples of which, with prices, they will be happy to send on application. Particular attention is called to their new specialities, The "Cameo," Royal Court "Azure," Original Treasury Parchment and London Grey, supplied in fashionable sizes.[1]

Meeting House Lane, not far from the Treacher emporium and skirting the dingy darkness of the South Lanes, also had more than its fair share of bookshops. In particular, number 9 seems to have changed hands quite regularly while always remaining well shelved. Alf Keeping had it from 1888 to 1898, then the Goddard brothers until 1902. John Richard Hitchings stepped in for a long stretch until 1924, when it passed to the Sandilands family, who seem to have moved up and down Meeting House Lane, trying out all kinds of retail businesses, for the next decade. Between them, the three Sandilands, J. F. and C., dealt in books, wardrobes, printing and dressmaking from numbers 9 and 18 until the beginning of the Second World War. There is a fine photograph in the Brighton History Centre archives of a stooping white-bearded gentleman with a rather fetching basket perusing ancient tomes tied up with string. He is outside Passe Partout, the Misses F. and C. Sandilands shop at number 18.

Back up on Queens Road, failing eyesight created a successful business. In 1839 at the early age of 21, a young man named William Moon lost his sight. He made it his life's work to invent and promote an embossed reading system that was simpler to use than Braille. The first work in 'Moon' type appeared in 1847 when the Moon Society was founded from his

---

[1] (unknown, Brighton and Hove Almanack, 1899)

home at 104 Queens Road. Further up the same street and obscured by countless wooden advertising hoardings, blind workers in the Moon Printing Works produced embossed books when production outgrew his private residence next door. In 1858 a 60 volume, 5,000 page Moon Bible was produced. Books and magazines in 471 languages were sent all over the world. When Dr. Moon died in 1894 his daughter, Adelaide, continued his work. While Braille has outlasted Moon's typography, the Brighton Society for the Blind have named their Hollingdean headquarters in his honour.[1] At the end of his long and productive life he retained an unshakeable Christian optimism: "It has been for me a long night, but a bright day."

SPECIMENS OF
Dr Moon's Type for the Blind
AS APPLIED TO FOREIGN LANGUAGES

English.
German.
Dutch.
Danish.
Swedish.
Russian.
Arabic.
Armenian.
Greek.

104. Queen's Road, Brighton.

---

[1] (Rutherford, 1898)

LIKE EVERYONE ELSE – Masons and Suicides

As a rule a bookshop is horribly cold in winter, because if it is too warm the windows get misted over, and a bookseller lives on his windows. And books give off more and nastier dust than any other class of objects yet invented, and the top of a book is the place where every bluebottle prefers to die[1].

At the beginning of the twentieth century, yet more bookshops arrived, some dealing in more specialist and esoteric subjects than popular general shops like D.B. Friend's. In 1919, John Metcalfe-Morton ran a shop at 1 Duke Street that dealt specifically in Masonic items and produced elaborate catalogues. This was always an expensive business so he advised customers, "when you have ordered all the books you want this time", to

---

[1] (Orwell, 1936)

pass the catalogues on to "a friend who is also interested, he will thank you to pass this list along to him – and so will Yours Truly." The shop was even called "Ye Olde Booke Shoppe" and sported the Lao Tzu motto "Be square without being angular". The Masons and Chinese philosophy: wrapped up, coincidentally, in anachronistic modern language. The alternative bookshops of the sixties and seventies would have enjoyed the synchronicity. No doubt Metcalfe-Morton derived a great deal of custom from the imposing and monolithic nineteenth-century Sussex Masonic Club in Queen's Road. The shop had closed in 1924, however, before the Masonic Temple next door to the club opened in 1928. Masons and interested parties could still visit an A. Metcalfe-Morton who dealt in similar items from 44 Gloucester Road by then.

Like so many places in Brighton, these premises had once been a pub, the Coach and Horses. Next, the Blue Arrow Book Company (run by a Mr. D. Morgan – "New Books, second-hand, remainders, catalogues, Scientific and Technical books stocked, Book Weeks[1]") took up residence before finally becoming known as the 'Old Bookhouse' for some years. This new Metcalfe-Morton and Morgan business flourished here from 1925 to around 1940. Stock at the 'Old Bookhouse' doubled in that time from 5000 to 10,000 items and included Masonica, Curios and Occult and antiquarian books. Naturally they ran a small circulating library as well. Thirty years later, at the other end of the same road, the imposing gay American, Bill Butler, would set up Brighton's first major alternative hippy emporium, the Unicorn Bookshop. What would he have made of the Occult and Masonica specialist down the road? And what would they have made of him?

In the middle of World War I Brighton received its largest ever injection of rare and valuable books. Bookshops, however, have never seen any of them and they are now public property. Leonard L. Bloomfield, inheritor of a successful military outfitters and embroiderers business based in London,

---

[1] (Philip, 1927)

passed away in Derbyshire, aged 59, in 1916. His house, a large villa in Withdean called Elme Lea, was stuffed with books "stacked in great piles on the floor". He had been a considerable collector of many types of rare book and his accumulated treasures ranged from unique manuscripts and incunabula to risqué nineteenth-century French paperbacks. As per his wishes, and no doubt in concert with her desires, his widow donated the entire collection –over 13,000 volumes in total– to the Brighton Public Library where they now form the core of the Rare Books and Special Collections on the upper floor of the Jubilee Library. With the men away at war, it was left to elderly librarians and young ladies to begin the long and arduous task of organizing, cataloguing and presenting the bequest. The *Brighton Herald* reported that the grateful but dazed library staff felt "as if the late Mr Bloomfield had hurled an avalanche of books at their heads." One of the young ladies on hand to help was a Miss Treacher. Books ran in the family's blood, it appears.

> "And here's the Charing Cross Road. This is where all the second-hand book shops are. Many's the hour I've spent poking about in some of these places; standing, sometimes, for the whole of lunch time, reading some book I couldn't afford to buy. Yes, you can stand there as long as you like, reading, and no one says a word." ...It revived memories of her trip down the Congo. A few old book-lovers, looking like those dull and crippled water insects which resemble bits of old dry stick, which, again, are exactly like book-lovers, hung precariously at the shop fronts, as if in fear of being swept away by the slowly drifting scum...
>
> - *His Monkey Wife* (or *Married to a Chimp*)
> John Collier 1930.

George 'Budd' Sexton's shops spread out from the north-west to the south-east, beginning in 1932 at 113 North Street, then a short shift to 110 and then to 14 Dyke Road. This last move did not entail much effort as the two addresses are in fact the same site, renamed and numbered by obscure civic juggling. Once again 14 Dyke Road was not innocent of bookish transactions either. In the previous decade it had been home to the Dials Lending Library. It remains a rather odd place, barely an address at all. It appears as a stepped crenelated protrusion from the southern end of the Gothic finery that is Wykeham Terrace and, like so many older Brighton bookshops, is very thin indeed. It has, despite George Orwell's recommendations above, no windows to speak of. As far as one can tell, after the renumbering and odd position of the shop, the premises must have gone a long way back, beside or under, number one Wykeham Terrace. Peter Sexton, George's grandson, remembers how cold the place was when he went there as a child and imagines it must once have been the kitchens for the nuns who ran a charitable institution there until 1912. This was St Mary's Home for Penitent Women, a Victorian euphemism for ex-prostitutes, set up in the 1850s.

Sexton finally settled down after another bookseller, James Thorpe, gave up his shop at 53 Ship Street. And a bookshop had been on *that* particular spot since 1868. The Dyke Road branch remained open and was a favourite of renowned book-dealer Anthony Rota. He remembers George Sexton's business partner: "Mr Morley lived a troglodyte's existence in cavern-like premises that were for the book-hunter a veritable Aladdin's cave."[1] George Sexton, who died at 83 in 1972, handed over the reins of his shops to his son, David.

Booksellers' memoirs come in two flavours. There are those that are written in despairing mood, concerned with the difficulties of changing economics and the decline of the trade and then there are jolly reminiscences of halcyon days spent drunk in the pleasant company of innumerable friends. In the

---

[1] (Rota, International League of Antiquarian Booksellers (ILAB), 2000)

year George Sexton died, David Low (in his *With All Faults*; a memoir of the second variety) remarked on the pleasures of this particular father/son handover: "This sense of continuity, and the passing on of old skills being one of the great charms of the antiquarian book trade."

Low's timing was unfortunate, as was his choice of bookshop, for two reasons. In 1978, the Ship Street branch finally closed: "Naturally I have certain regrets that this old established family business has closed down...[B]ut I have no-one to follow me into the business – so I'm afraid that's it,"[1] concluded David Sexton.

Low also chooses not to mention the fate of Edward Morley and 14 Dyke Road. That branch bore little resemblance to Aladdin's cave on the night of 18th January 1970. Police and Segas officials had to break the door down after neighbours in Gothic Towers, the terraced houses in Wykeham Terrace next to the premises, reported a gas leak. Morley was found in an alcove of the shop with a hose from an open gas pipe on his chest. His troglodyte existence consisted of more than simply haunting the shop at all hours. He was 65 and very sick but refused to go to hospital, his wife reported at the inquest. He had money worries too. His full name was Edwin Gaius Morley and, in the traditionally dispassionate words of the coroner, he "took his life while the balance of his mind was disturbed."

The seventies were not all about sad ends to the Sexton story though. In a twist that only Brighton could provide, David Sexton, from the long-established and traditional book trade, was friends with Bill Butler, the American beat poet and owner of the Unicorn alternative bookshop in Gloucester Road from 1968 to 1974. And despite David's comments in 1978, his son Peter still deals in books on the internet to this day.

After Sexton, though, and sparked perhaps by 'Ye Olde Booke Shoppe', a Masonic divide of bookshops formed: an esoteric angle of bookish thoroughfares. Trafalgar Street and Duke Street/Ship Street/North Street to the north and south

---

[1] Reported in the *Argus*, 1 Dec. 1978.

respectively, with Queen's Road, from the station to the sea, providing a third side. Preparing the way, a Thomas Tourle dealt books from 19 Trafalgar Street while E. J. Trill and Trill & Son worked from 7 Duke Street and 22 Duke Street as booksellers and publishers (these three as early as 1889). S.W. Tidy was in Ship Street in 1927 (and established in 1912) and J. Jordan's 'People's Books' in Trafalgar Street in 1950 while Doris Strong was at 13 Duke Street, along with the indomitable Holleyman & Treacher. As for the eastern arm, Grand Parade, the Steines Old and New: there the square was broken open, the exchange of books perhaps hampered by the elaborate Royal etiquette of the Pavilion or the hidden course of the Wellesbourne (now underground and culverted into the sea) running invisibly around the megaliths dumped here from St Nicholas' church on Dyke Road or the fabled Goldstone stone circle. Bookshops did not spring up there, as the old libraries had over a century before. Pool Valley could still flood during bad storms back then and eventually Aleister Crowley's cremated ashes washed back into the heart of the town from the Downs where they were scattered. Fire and water, the elemental enemies of books.

The point of poetic licence is that it is not strictly true. From 1918 W.F. Fowler, who liked to specialise in French literature (Cowper Powys might have been interested had he still been around), had eight thousand books to sell in precisely that area. However, his tiny run-down eighteenth-century cottage at 18 Marlborough Place, next to the King & Queen pub, only lasted until 1935. In that year his shop, a large chunk of the entire row and the old frontage of the pub was demolished and replaced, leaving no trace of the wooden fence and the few steps down from the pavement to a dark shop whose sign announced 'Curios, Old China, Engravings, Books & Works of Art, Bought, Sold or Exchanged, Good Prices Given'. Even later, at the same address but with an entirely different face, 'The Marlborough Bookshop', run by W. Torrens-Burton, established in 1976 and lasting until the early eighties, continued alone in that part of town.

Other booksellers' strategic positioning makes a good deal more sense. Where else could you put 'The Theatre Bookshop' but in New Road, almost opposite the Theatre Royal? Established by Miss J.E. Tee in 1962, this three-storey shop specialised in what you might expect along with private press books and antiquarian rarities. It changed hands in later years and was called 'Atkinson-Ryman'. The shop finally closed in the late seventies.

Miss Tee was one of the many widows who became friendly with a dealer in books and antiques named Townley. He had no shop but kept several lock-up stores around town, buying and selling to shops and other dealers when the time and the price were right. Townley was not so astute when it came to paying rent, however. At one time a store of his books was sold as a job lot by a landlord to cover what he was owed. These books, a rather good selection as it turned out, eventually began turning up at the Sunday car-boot fair held in the Brighton Station car park to the delight and astonishment of several book scouts who hurried back into town to sell off their finds.

However, Miss Tee was not the first bookseller in New Road. That honour went to Richard H. Quinton Edwards as far as I can gather. He was at 32 New Road in 1927 and then seems to have blossomed in many places and under many variations on a name. By 1936 he was at 14c Dyke Road - but so was the Dials Library, run by V. McLean. The 'Q' Circulating Libraries, owned by a Richard H. Edwards and founded in 1933 and 1934, were at 45 North Street. And in Tunbridge Wells. And the Quinton Edwards Bookshop - new books, general fiction, juvenile, Book Tokens, fancy goods, window space and Christmas shows - took pride of place in New Road.

There was no stopping him. By 1950 'Quinton Edwards' was also at Boscombe, Tonbridge and Worthing. But then, sometime in the fifties, it all disappears.

Today, at east and west extremes, the independents hold sway: Kemp Town Books in, well, Kemp Town and City Books along Western Road, are excellent shops with a great deal of local community support. Others have fallen by the wayside.

Practical Books in Western Road belied its name by specialising in books on spirituality upstairs while concealing a dingy and somewhat battered and confusing basement of second-hand stock. In existence since 1963, it finally closed after 40 years in 2003, a victim of rent increases. The business, run during its final four years by Yvonne Norman, was not alone. When asked what she would do next, she said that she had considered moving to Spain, "like everyone else."[1]

There was an excellent central independent once. The much-missed Read All About It began in St James's Street but ended up in East Street and was finally forced to close during the Net Book Agreement wars of the mid-nineties when discounting on the Recommended Retail Price (RRP) of books allowed supermarkets to take a chunk of the market, the US giant Borders to invade and books to become cheaper than ever before[2]. However, independent bookshops could not compete with the economic clout of big chain retailers and, since the Agreement was declared illegal (as price-fixing) in 1997, over 500 smaller shops across the country have been forced to close. The owners of Read All About It posted a reasoned but understandably bitter note about this turn of events in the

---

[1] Argus report, August 2003
[2] So too was the Blackwells in Bond Street, now Clarkes Stationers. A new branch is hidden away at the heart of the University of Brighton on Lewes Road.

windows of the shop when it finally closed. Philip Reeve, author of the wonderful *Mortal Engines*[1] series, worked there for a time.

> The personal service and ordering facilities that we offered haven't been enough to save us, price cutting unfortunately beating what we believed to be quality bookselling[2].

---

[1] *Mortal Engines, Predators Gold, Infernal Devices* (which features a cutting, and therefore entirely accurate, portrayal of Brighton and its cultures) and *A Darkling Plain*.
[2] Proprietors David and Cathy Dale, reported in the *Argus*, 19 Jun. 1997.

THE FILTH – Bill Butler and the Unicorn Bookshop

For the release of Alan Sinfield's *Wilde Century* in 1994, Read All About It devoted a major window display to gay and lesbian literature and history, a field in which the town is justifiably renowned. Unfortunately, however, East Street is not far from the Brighton Centre, and that vast concrete establishment is equally well-known for hosting regular Evangelical Christian conferences. When these two events successfully managed to coincide, certain religiously inclined visitors were summarily outraged and complaints were made to the shop. But gay icons Abba had won the Eurovision song contest at the Brighton Centre itself in 1974: did these people have no sense of history? And this was only one of many in a long series of fault-line antagonisms that cause dark spaces to appear between Brighton and its books. Back in the 1960s the staff at the Unicorn Bookshop would not have been impressed by such outrageous bigotry. Nor, I'm sure, would any of the staff and owners of Solstice, Public House Bookshop, Symposium, Avalon Books or the Odd Volume.

It must be admitted that there is no dedicated lesbian and gay bookshop in Brighton currently[1]. Out!, founded by Chris and Richard Farrah-Mills in Dorset Street, closed way back in 2001 and the only spaces to take its place have been the generic sections in Waterstone's and any shop with sufficient grasp of local custom to capitalise on what is a surprising omission in a town of Brighton's size and reputation.

But what diverse bookshops has Brighton seen?

Here are the booksellers who fill in the gaps between the mysterious 'Q' libraries, the staggering behemoth of Waterstone's and the two surviving independent bookshops of today.

But, as is so often the case, the easiest way to irritate Brighton is to start in London.

During the hot summer of 1971 three defendants were tried at the Old Bailey in London under the Obscene Publications Act. It was the longest obscenity trial in history[2]. Richard Neville was the editor of OZ magazine, a lively, stimulating and regularly unreadable alternative newspaper. Several issues had been devoted to what we might now call single issue politics: a feminist issue edited by Germaine Greer, a gay issue and a flying saucer issue ("...not edited by little green men"). Then the editors had the brilliant idea of handing the magazine over to adolescents, just in case they might appear out of touch with the youth: the result was the School Kids Issue. Neville was the grand old age of 30 at the time of the trial. This issue of the magazine landed them in the dock; that pesky line in

---

[1] I would love to be wrong about this...
[2] All this information and a good deal more can be found in Tony Palmer's invaluable but painfully exhaustive account of the entire event, *The Trials of OZ*, Blond & Briggs 1971. It was however published before the appeal against the sentences some months later.

the Act about a tendency "to deprave and corrupt persons" and the possibility of a "conspiracy to corrupt public morals". In these more cynical times it might appear remarkable that the Law Courts and the unreconstructed Constabulary would have the temerity to call that particular kettle black but, as the saying goes, things were different then.

Neville, an Australian, had started a version of OZ in his native land where it had already been prosecuted for obscenity. But that verdict was subsequently quashed on appeal. This time more was at stake and things, as everyone on both sides later agreed, were to get out of hand. It became by far the most public stand of the alternative press in Britain and certainly exhibited all the hallmarks of two cultures at loggerheads. John Mortimer QC, author of the 'Rumpole of the Bailey' series, defended two of the accused. Neville, in true hippy style, did not want to use the services of the Law and defended himself. An appeal fund raised £6000. Artists and performers lined up to speak for the defendants: George Melly, Professor H.J. Eysenck, Marty Feldman, John Peel, Edward de Bono and Caroline Coon to name only a few. Not all of them were as helpful to the case as perhaps OZ would have liked but that is missing the point. John Lennon wrote a song about it. Demonstrators with placards lined the streets of London while in the courtroom the sight of British justice, slow, ill-informed and pedantic, wearing numbingly away at three hippies, was painful to see and unedifying to say the least.

At the close, the three defendants were found not guilty on the conspiracy charge but guilty on several other counts. The Judge in the case handed down some exorbitant sentences, including that Richard Neville be deported. Appeals were made, the Judge was reprimanded and, finally, the convictions were, once again, quashed[1].

---

[1] In fact, the obvious unfairness of this trial and its initial outcome is cited as a significant motivating factor in a major police corruption trial that resulted in multiple convictions and the jailing for 10 years of the senior officer responsible for the original prosecution (OZ trial lifted lid on porn squad bribery – Alan Travis, Nov 13th 1999, Guardian Unlimited website).

With hindsight it is easier to put these culture clashes in perspective. In America the hippies were already on their way out. Altamont had ruined their much-vaunted inclusivity and peaceful ardour. The alternative culture was already packaged and awaiting endless consumption. OZ itself, along with rivals *International Times* and Neville's own new *Ink*, while perhaps hoping to struggle up the ladder to bigger readerships and circulations, soon fell away. OZ folded in 1973. Journalists would get their start in the alternative press but could be lured away by money and, it must be said, significant editorial policy changes in the mainstream. One of the school kid contributors to the OZ issue in question was Charles Shaar Murray who went on to write so brilliantly for the NME. Edges soon blur. The Establishment is slow, but it can learn, much to the annoyance of revolutionaries. Idealism can meet pragmatism halfway.

But hindsight takes away the values of the moment, the individual stories. These people had no money but they did have the enormous support of a visible and vocal minority. There was the zeitgeist to consider. It was news.

Three years earlier, in 'London-by-the-Sea', court cases didn't quite reach such epic heights of cultural significance. However, they could still match the capital for ignorance and vindictiveness.

> And just because books are the repository of all the redemptions and damnations, all the sanities and insanities, of the divine anarchy of the soul, they are still, as they have always been, an object of suspicion to every kind of ruling authority[1].

Initially William Huxford Butler couldn't seem to sort things out. Born in Washington, USA, in 1934, he dropped out, joined the marines, got married, had a child, got divorced,

---

[1] (Cowper Powys, The Pleasures of Literature, 1938)

worried about his homosexuality, worked as a fire-fighter, then as a radio announcer and attempted suicide. He arrived in London via most of Europe and worked in Better Books, Charing Cross Road. He wrote poetry and had an interest in the occult. Then, in 1965, he and his partner Michael Hughes moved to 12 Over Street in Brighton.

> I started dealing in books from my living room and at one time I was arse deep in books. This guy came round one day who said "My tenants aren't paying rent; I'm going to boot them out, the shop's round the corner. Do you want to rent a shop for a while?[1]

The Unicorn Bookshop at 50 Gloucester Road is a largely forgotten gem of Brighton's cultural history. Perhaps Brighton, if it exists as some kind of incorporeal psychogeographic entity, finds its treatment of the shop and Bill slightly embarrassing. Directly opposite (in more ways than one) the austere Regency façade of the Galeed Baptist Chapel, the shop on the corner with Frederick Street had been painted by artist John Upton with rainbows, the moon and stars and the rising sun. A fine prancing Unicorn projected from the second floor out over the pavement. In those days the road was open to traffic from the Queen's Road end and was busier than it is now. Unicorn popped up at just the right time to begin selling OZ and *International Times*. They catered for all things underground: posters, hippy beads, bells, US beat poetry magazines and contemporary fiction. This was one of the first and very few places where a reader could peruse from America the *Evergreen Review*, *Kulchur*, the *Los Angeles Free Press*, Olympia Press publications, the writings of William Burroughs, Jack Kerouac, Allen Ginsberg and Lawrence Ferlinghetti. In the here and now I imagine all the things Unicorn sold are thinly spread over almost every shop in Brighton. Back then, though, the shop was a focal

---

[1] (unknown, Bill Butler: Another sort of publisher, 1972)

point, selling the concentrated essence of the changing times. From selling and printing posters, Butler moved into publishing. Many poets saw the light of day thanks to Bill Butler and both J.G. Ballard and Michael Moorcock published some of their earlier work there.

> ...sunny Brighton days when it was definitely like S[an]F[rancisco] and the shop was one of the hubs of the scene. Bill and Michael would want all of life to be expressed in their world; they were true libertarians and there was such a strong head and alternative scene in the late 60s.[1]

This was all a far cry from the dowdy Victorian monoliths of blind and secret society just up on Queen's Road. The only 'competition' in the vicinity would have been Rossmore Express Books of 117 Queen's Road, huddling next to the huge Oddfellows Hall. It was no contest. The Hall and the building housing Express Books were demolished in August 1969. Before that, though, there were struggles to endure.

On January 16th 1968 three freshly-minted copies of Ballard's *Why I Want to Fuck Ronald Reagan* were sitting quietly in the Unicorn Bookshop in a sealed envelope addressed to Mrs Anne Graham-Bell, then head of Public Relations for Penguin Books. This short piece, published as a chapbook by Unicorn, subsequently became part of the novel *The Atrocity Exhibition*, published by Jonathan Cape in 1970 and described by the Sunday Telegraph as "a powerful, uneasy book". Ballard is now, without a shadow of a doubt, seen as one of the most important writers of the 20th century:

---

[1] Personal reminiscence from the 'Bookshops' thread at www.mybrightonandhove.org.uk.

> **Apocalypse.** A disquieting feature of this annual exhibition – to which the patients themselves were not invited – was the marked preoccupation of the paintings with the theme of world cataclysm, as if these long-incarcerated patients had sensed some seismic upheaval within the minds of their doctors and nurses.
>
> - J. G. Ballard – *The Atrocity Exhibition*

At midday on the 16th four Brighton policemen entered the building and told the manager, poet Lee Harwood, that the shop was closed. They proceeded to search the premises for three and a half hours, eventually leaving with three thousand, two hundred and forty-one items of stock. The police referred to what they had taken as 'obscenity' under the Obscene Publications Act of 1959. The envelope for Mrs Graham-Bell was part of this haul. The police later denied that they had closed the shop despite having already thrown customers out and refused access to Butler's solicitor (who only got in after an argument). Were there people in the Baptist Chapel watching as four policemen carted this huge pile of obscenity down the road to a waiting police van?

So began an unedifying chapter in Brighton's long relationship with the underground[1]. In an effort to treat the entire town as simply a larger version of Folthorp's 'Library for the Young' from over a century earlier, the Establishment proceeded to prove that "great care [would be] taken to exclude all publications of an immoral or doubtful tendency" from its supposedly pristine environs.

There had been portents before this storm broke. Eight months earlier, a boy helping to run the shop had been picked up elsewhere on a charge of possessing cannabis and sent to Borstal. Another helper, David Field, was arrested while reading

---

[1] (Hollis, 2009)

an Allen Ginsberg poem to 200 people on Brighton beach. This performance had been officially sanctioned and was a regular event. In that case, the chairman of the magistrates, Mr John Cuttress, said that "there was no evidence of annoyance to the public by the use of a word which was part of a published work by a recognised poet," and dismissed the case.[1] Imagine the annoyance of a 200-strong audience at having your speaker hastened away by policemen in the middle of a reading. But that's not the point.

Lee Harwood remembers a petty reason why the police may not have been enamoured of the bookshop. Sometime before the raid, a local officer had been charged with stealing women's underwear from washing lines in Whitehawk. Bill, adapting the famous warning notice of the time, quickly ran up a poster of a silhouetted officer sneaking away with a bra: "Watch Out, Watch Out, There's a Copper About".

> 27. A barrister has advised me that in his view the Brighton police probably have it in for me. It has been suggested that the shop might be better off in London.[2]
>
> I think it's fuzz harassment. The *International Times* is dangerous. Unicorn is dangerous. We've got paper bombs.[3]

An over-sensitive constabulary and a provocative bookshop owner in a town concerned for its reputation.

The emergence of 'alternative' bookshops and their ensuing difficulties had already been noted in the wider trade world. Martin Parnell, co-founder of the Trent Bookshop in Nottingham in 1965, had summed up the relevant issues at a library symposium only a year before. Unicorn, and later OZ,

---

[1] 'Unicorn Hunt in Brighton' – The Guardian, 2 Sept 1968
[2] From Bill Butler's typed notes before the trial.
[3] Bill Butler, *International Times* 24, Jan 19th-Feb 1st 1968 – just after the raid.

when maliciously brought to the attention of the general public, did not find a liberal or receptive response, no matter what their artistic and optimistic defences.

> In connection with my point about the stock, whatever has been said in the papers about censorship, one of the most obnoxious forms of censorship exercised in this country is the non-availability of hundreds of titles because general booksellers either do not stock them or refuse to do so because of their supposed pornographic or obscene content. Bookshops, and that means places like Better Books, Indica, the Old Zwemmers, all in London, are naturally meeting places for the arts, where people should be able to meet and discuss with novelists, poets, critics, painters, the latest books, paintings etc. They should give rise to other activities – publishing, readings, talks, events, happenings and encourage people who are ignored by the commercial interests of big business.[1]

John Mortimer QC, the man who would go on to defend the OZ editors, had already contributed an introduction to *Books in the Dock*, which called for serious changes to the 1959 Obscene Publications Act. The author highlights the problems with many famous literary obscenity trials: *Lady Chatterley*, *Last Exit to Brooklyn*, Henry Miller, Norman Mailer and the exploits of the notorious nineteenth-century pornographer, Edmund Curll. Mortimer, Butler and Cowper Powys are once again all thinking along the same lines about the power of books:

> Writers should no doubt, if they ever stop to think about it, feel complimented by the fact

---

[1] (Parnell, 1968)

that so many people, in and out of authority, regard all print with deep fear and suspicion. Words are seen as unexploded mines...[1]

Butler was denied legal aid three times. After five days in court and expert testimony from John Pudney, writer, Eric Mottram, University lecturer, Anthony Godwin, editor and publisher, Ann Graham-Bell of Penguin Books, George MacBeth, poet and BBC producer[2] and Dr Arnold Goldman, Lecturer in English and American Studies at the University of Sussex (who all ably explained the importance to students of literature and sociology of the works retained by the police), Mr Michael Worsley, prosecuting counsel, appeared intellectually unmoved. "The magistrates will know a dirty book when they see one," he said. Well, yes. Quite.

The Chairman of the Magistrates was the exquisitely named Mr Herbert J. Ripper[3], a retired Labour Exchange manager, who was joined on the bench by an auctioneer's wife and a car salesman and garage proprietor. In Brighton, in a Magistrates court, there was no jury to win over as there was to be in the OZ case. Just these three upstanding members of the local community, a community that may well have been under economic pressure to avoid any whiff of controversy in a pleasant seaside town desperate for summer tourism. Brighton's reputation appeared to be at stake again. First Graham Greene, then those Mods and Rockers, and now this. Where would it all end? Books and young people simply don't do Brighton any good, do they?

---

[1] (Rolph, 1969)
[2] And, perhaps ironically, author of 'The Virgin's Prayer' and 'The Pornography Poem' in *Ambit 34* published that same year.
[3] The Prosecutor in the OZ trial three years later was called Mr Leary, a name finely balanced between petty voyeuristic lewdness, which the trial successfully generated, and the massive enlightening drug experiences of Timothy. Mr Ripper had a less equivocal moniker.

So, despite support from the young and radical University of Sussex, eminent publishers and noted academics, Bill Butler was fined £250 plus 180 guineas costs. His legal fees were £1000 and the value of the confiscated material was around £2000. Eighty books were burnt and most of those remaining were newspapers, like OZ, that were by now worthless. It seems that Brighton certainly was "appalled at the filth that has been produced in this court", as Mr Ripper claimed, but was quite happy about book burning.

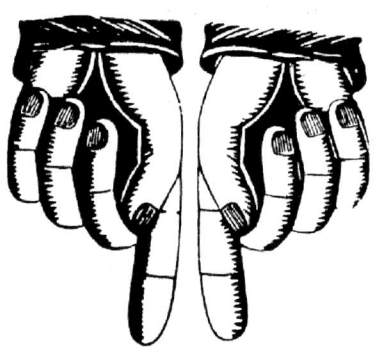

RIPPER, RIPPER BURNING BRIGHT
BOOKS TOO DARK FOR HUMAN SIGHT;
DOESN'T ALL THAT FILTHY MUCK
MAKE YOU WANT TO WANK & FUCK,
RIPPER, RIPPER TELL ME RIGHT
WHICH IS FILTH & WHICH DELIGHT.

This debt was a serious business for a small bookshop and press with little or no money in the bank and providing "only a marginal living", as even the Court allowed. It is unlikely that Butler ever really paid off the full amount. Arnold Goldman, who gave evidence at the trial, circulated a supportive petition and promoted the Unicorn Defence Fund, based in London. Goldman was as appalled by the magistrate's general attitude to the academics who had defended the shop and the works in question as he was by the outcome of the trial. Sussex was a new and progressive University while Brighton was still a town struggling to find an identity.

> When Unicorn started it was the only thing in Brighton. Since then there's about 6-8 places and a lot of people working down there, so far with very little direction; they very seldom come together. There's not much sense of

actual community. The word community is used frequently in Brighton. It's used by each one of us differently. It's a much more active and interesting place than it was, but it has the advantage over London that it's still slower.[1]

Unicorn received hate mail over the trial period. One was simply of the "dirty hippy, get a job" variety but the second is slightly stranger. Written on toilet paper it was obviously sent by someone who had been following the trial and was aware of a turn of phrase Butler had used in his defence concerning 'truth'. This was also someone who should have spent more time brushing up on their grammar and less time checking out Unicorn's apparently provocative window displays: "Take that there book out, or I tell the police, again on Saturday. The Naked Woman 2/6 knocked down to 1/6 written on her naked back. Out or else, there'll be another Obscene Case you. You'll feel the chill of truth too." The last two sentences are not entirely legible, though the sentiment is clear enough.

On a more positive note, there had also been a letter of appeal sent out to sympathetic writers that resulted, by early 1970, in the collection *For Bill Butler*, edited by Eric Mottram and Larry Wallrich. Designed to help defray some of Butler's costs and to draw attention to "one of the most savage exposures of the ignorance, superciliousness and illiteracy of Establishment opinion this country has heard," this limited edition of five hundred emerged only a year after the more famous *Children of Albion: Poetry of Underground Britain* (Penguin 1969), edited by Michael Horowitz. *For Bill Butler* featured work by sixteen of the UK poets in *...Albion*, including Horowitz himself, while also embracing Jeff Nuttall, Bob Cobbing, George Macbeth, Elaine Feinstein, Thom Gunn, the Liverpool poets and such US figures as Ginsberg, Tuli Kupferberg and Ted Berrigan.

Britain's staid and respectable "Establishment opinion" seems to have been exceptionally irritable in the middle of 1968,

---

[1] (unknown, Bill Butler: Another sort of publisher, 1972)

while Unicorn was on trial. Michael Moorcock had recently taken over *New Worlds* science-fiction magazine and was turning it into a vibrant and revolutionary outlet for new and experimental work. They were serialising an original novel by the American SF author Norman Spinrad, called *Bug Jack Barron*, when, in March, their main distributors, W. H. Smith, decided to pull the latest issue, arguing that it was obscene. Once again, it is hardly worth mentioning that the assessment is, at best, debatable, let alone questioning when, why and how Smith's had decided to appoint themselves as cultural judges for the country as a whole. This High Street ban was reported in the press and a question was asked in the House of Commons as to why the Arts Council was "sponsoring filth"[1]. The Establishment seemed to be taking every opportunity to make life difficult for Moorcock, along with his friends and colleagues. Filth, apparently, was everywhere.

As to *Why I Want to Fuck Ronald Reagan*, Ballard sensibly said nothing publicly. According to Moorcock, Ballard did not want to go to court as the piece "was intentionally obscene and, if called, would have to say so"[2]. To argue about such things one way or the other would be to miss a significant point in Ballard's work after all. In fact, a few years later that section of *The Atrocity Exhibition* still led to the entire initial Doubleday print run being pulped in the United States when the President of that company (and a friend of the actor, governor and later US President) made the mistake of actually reading one of his own publications[3]. It was finally published by Grove Press, home to William Burroughs and other avant-garde writers, whose works could be found, at least most the time, in the Unicorn Bookshop at 50 Gloucester Road, Brighton.

> Fortunately men like Bill Butler may be **put** down - but never **kept** down. The quicker he

---

[1] (Ashley, 2005)
[2] Michael Moorcock - J.G. Ballard obituary in Timesonline, April 25 2009
[3] (Ballard, 2008)

is restored to a position where he can function freely and fully as artist and publisher and proprietor the better off the world of letters will be. One would expect better of England, where we have so often looked in the past for liberal leadership of spirit.[1]

Bill was an imposing figure; well over 6ft with a shock of blond hair over a craggy face with deep blue areas beneath his eyes that made him look like he'd been up all night. In fact he used to get up at 6am to write fuelled by some of the strongest tea I've ever seen and would often go to bed early – he may have been an insomniac. He was highly strung – most charming one moment and in a rage the next. When raging he was quite intimidating and would bear down on people in an attempt to get his way. I remember hearing of him throwing a crate of empty milk bottles to the ground outside the shop in a fit of rage.

- Stefan Szczelkun

Unicorn did continue. Despite the troubles, it remained a meeting place for many important counter-culture figures. Allen Ginsberg visited from the US, as did William Burroughs during his stay in London during the early seventies. Butler published *Ali's Smile* by Burroughs in 1971 and Eric Mottram's study *Allen Ginsberg in the Sixties*. Roy Pennington, later a local Brighton Councillor, put together a limited edition collection of Burroughs' columns in *Mayfair* magazine from Unicorn. Poet and long-term Brighton resident Lee Harwood worked there for a time and Jeff Nuttall was a regular visitor. Nuttall's collection *Love Poems* appeared under the Unicorn

---

[1] Ronald H. Bayes – Writer-in-Residence, St. Andrews College, Laurinburg, North Carolina, USA: (Wallrich, 1970)

imprint. Doreen Valiente, another Brighton local, author of numerous books on modern witchcraft[1] and probably the most important white witch from the second half of the twentieth century, no doubt discussed occult matters at the shop with Butler. Unicorn also published S.L Macgregor Mathers' short notes on the Tarot. Mathers was one of the original and certainly the most significant founder of the Order of the Golden Dawn, a Victorian magical society whose members, at one time or another, included W.B. Yeats and Aleister Crowley. Crowley died along the coast, at Hastings, in 1947 but was cremated at Brighton. It is a little known fact that all books about Brighton are legally obliged to mention Crowley. Butler's own critically acclaimed work on the Tarot, *The Definitive Tarot*, was published by Rider in 1975.

Another literary figure that must always be mentioned in connection with Brighton is Graham Greene. Incongruous as it might first appear, one of Greene's favourite bookshops of Brighton in the early seventies was Unicorn. He took his friend, and professional book-dealer, David Low to the "meaner streets downhill [from the station]" where they met "...the owner, a young American in jeans, who had given up Californian sun, the sands, and palms of the Pacific, for the grey English Channel and the shingle, but he said that he loved it all."[2] Low notes the presence of a little ginger cat as well, which seems to have been a favourite of Bill's, as well as "rows of forgotten early twentieth-century authors," which were less than interesting to the experienced dealer.

The alternative papers were supplied by a new underground press distributor called Frit Freight, run by Paul Garner and some friends. Once again, Bill made a big impression.

---

[1] Including *An ABC of Witchcraft* (1973) and *Natural Magic* (1975). She died at Brighton in 1999, aged seventy-seven.
[2] (Low, 1973)

> One day, I suppose it was early summer 1969 and within a few weeks of starting our business, there came a knock on the door at Camelot, Frit Freight's centre of ops, a bungalow near The Mount, in Guildford. It was a tall stranger, looking like a frontiersman in jeans and fringed jacket. An unannounced and unexpected Bill Butler came in, and, making himself right at home, sat on the floor, leaned back against the fireplace, hand rolled a cigarette and said: "now this is where it's at..."
>
> Bill proceeded to tell us all about what I later came to call "the social, cultural, and political context" in which we were working; the world according to Bill. He was of course "right on"![1]

The late Patrick Newley remembers working in the shop as a young man and is also one of the few who mentions Butler's sexuality and its effect on the bookshop, something that is missing, perhaps significantly, from any papers on the trial.

> He was about six foot seven, he looked like John Wayne and lived with his lover. No-one would ever have thought, for a second, that he was gay. He used to wear a great big stetson hat and had a wicked sense of humour. We'd sell the ordinary books like *The Naked Lunch*, *The Politics of Ecstasy* and things like that, but we'd always throw in a couple of gay books as well. It was amazing, the number of people that used to write in for *City of Night* by John Rechy or Numbers or something like that. They might put a little PS and say, 'Do you have any more books of the same type?' In other words,

---

[1] Paul Garner - personal communication.

they were screaming old queens who wanted more gay books. We used to recommend *Our Lady of the Flowers* and *Funeral Rites* by Genet... But we used to get dirty old men coming in, thinking that *The Naked Lunch* was going to give them a good time for a toss off and then, of course, they'd read it and they couldn't understand a fucking word.[1]

Reversing Butler's moves, Newley left Unicorn for London and worked in Better Books for John Calder before going on to a varied career as broadcaster, press agent and theatrical management

Along with his poetry connections, Butler wrote and moved in science fiction circles too. In 1973 the 'Unicorn Fantasy' series published *The Jade Man's Eyes, Elric: The Return to Melniboné* by Michael Moorcock, and later the 'Jerry Cornelius' science-fiction pastiche *The Distant Suns* in 1975, co-written and illustrated by Jim Cawthorn. With Ballard and Moorcock of the *New Worlds* crew, he was a friend of the American poet and SF author Thomas M. Disch. Like Butler, Disch was a gay man who made little overt reference to his sexuality in his writings.[2] In 1968 both Butler and Disch, along with the other usual suspects, appeared in a contemporary, though somewhat quaintly titled, SF anthology, which must have been a pleasant if minor respite from the travails of that year.[3] Certainly not modern but no less in touch with the zeitgeist, Unicorn also brought back into print one of William Morris's more obscure fantasy novels, *The Sundering Flood*, first published in 1897.

However, Butler's abiding interest was the alternative society. Unicorn published a series called the *Survival Scrapbooks*

---

[1] (Newley, Daring Hearts: Lesbian and Gay Lives of 50s and 60s Brighton, 1992)
[2] "I'm gay myself but I don't write 'gay' literature." – interview in *Strange Horizons*, 2001
[3] *England Swings SF* - Edited by Judith Merrill, Doubleday 1968/Ace Books 1970. Ironically, there does not appear to have been a UK edition. Bill's story was called 'The First Gorilla on the Moon'.

initially written by Stefan A. Szcelkun: *Part 1-Shelter*, *Part 2-Food*, *Part 3-Access to Tools* (Williams and Munro). Following these came *Part 4-Urban Alternatives*, *Part 5-Paper Houses* ("How to build a house for £200 or £500 that you can walk out of like you do your blue jeans") and *Part 6-Energy As Power* ("Energy in all forms: physical, psychic. A long enough lever to move the earth"). At least, these are the proposed descriptions advertised in other Unicorn publications. What actually appeared seems to have been *Part 3½ - Play*, *Part 4* was *Paper Houses*, *Part 5 – Energy* and 6 never made it into print. The actual achievements of small press publishing sometimes fail to live up to their ambitions, turning bibliographies into a minefield.[1] The early *Survival Scrapbooks* have recently appeared in an ecological exhibition in Liverpool[2], prime examples of an easily forgotten history of green activism.

The Infinity Foods co-operative started up in 1971 at a terraced house in Church Street and is still going strong today in new and expanded premises on North Road. Butler published their first book, *Nature's Foods*, by the co-operative's founder, Pete Deadman. He remembers Unicorn forming part of a "tiny coterie of hippy businesses in the early 70's" that included Infinity, the Public House Bookshop in Little Preston Street and Ananda (again, still a business in Brighton but now specialising in ethnic furniture in Bond Street). Butler even published his own local paper/freak mag. According to *Alternative Brighton*, published in 1974, edited by John Noyce and, of course, printed by Unicorn, *Attila* "came out regularly under several editors...producing 40 issues in all in the first series." *Attila* ran from May 1971 until June 1973. So there was still a lot to say and do.[3]

By 1972, though, Butler admitted that the times had changed.

---

[1] Two bibliographies of Unicorn productions have been underway for some years now, though neither has yet seen the light of day.
[2] 'Climate for Change', 13 March to 31 May 2009, organised by FACT, the Foundation for Art and Creative Technology.
[3] *The Underground and Alternative Press in Britain during 1975*, Harvester Press 1977, compiled by William Puddick with John Noyce as Contributing Editor.

It went from that very open, friendly, believing thing, which didn't last long, maybe a year or so, to become more and more political and the political thing came to a head, or so it seemed from Brighton, last year. The edge of it has gone off now. You know, I think the underground papers in London are dead. Either dead or going to change a hell of a lot. They're either going to become more consumer orientated, like *Nasty Tales*, or they're going to die, like OZ. I think the recent issue was maybe the last. It was certainly very together, and had a swan-song feel about it.[1]

It wasn't all sweetness and light either. Underground poets and authors were only too pleased to be published at all, especially by an imprint with connections like Unicorn. Little things like contracts, publication dates and actual cash were for the straights. Before the disillusionment with Brighton, Lee Harwood knew Bill from Better Books in London and performance poet Bob Cobbings' poetry workshops. In 1969 he was in New York when he got a call from Bill asking if he would like to come back and run the shop for a while so that Bill could concentrate on poster printing ventures and his interests in the occult. Lee, who was enjoying New York, decided it would only be worthwhile if he could run the shop to his own design; stocking a wide selection of poetry and interesting new work: a new, better, Better Books. Of course, Bill agreed.

But the finances never quite flowed and Bill's hand hovered for hours over pay cheques in some kind of power game. He would turn up with boxes of his own occult-related purchases while never quite allowing Lee the free rein he had been promised. After about three months Lee found himself opening the shop, looking around the cluttered little space and thinking,

---

[1] (unknown, Bill Butler: Another sort of publisher, 1972)

what the hell am I doing? He locked up, went round to Bill's flat in Over Street and posted the keys through the door. Several other people managed the shop over the next few years, including another US ex-pat, Richard Cupidi.

And sometimes it went a little further than simply a relaxed, laid-back (but irritating) attitude to business. When the *Survival Scrapbooks* became a successful underground publishing phenomenon, three of them were reprinted in the US by Schocken Books[1] and sold well. Butler kept the subsequent royalties (owed to the author) and embarked on a major change in his life and work.

And so, in 1973, the owners of the Unicorn Bookshop finally left Brighton. Bill and the press moved to a remote cottage in Wales, a place called Nant Gwilw. Michael Hughes, his partner, went with him, as did Tony Bennett and Malcolm, yet another ex-manager of the shop "...to carry on an unfortunately short-lived co-operative publishing and self-sufficiency experiment where we printed all our own books, and sat around in the evenings collating and binding them while sipping from liquor of varying strengths, ranging from just passable to 'what have I done to myself?' all produced from our own still."[2] Tony Bennett had hung around Unicorn since it opened. Bill took him on to do some book-keeping for the shop, then he moved into cover design and also edited some Crowley titles that Bill was working on (*The Book of the Law*, *Liber Aleph* and *The Soldier and the Hunchback* among others).

With a couple involved who ran the farming side of things, this little commune continued to produce books from the printing press in the barn while growing their own food and learning a little animal husbandry. It was here that Unicorn published the Infinity Foods book, along with *Wild Foods of Great Britain* and more in the Survival Scrapbooks series. *Rudiments of Tabla Playing*, *Klingsohr's Fairy Tale* by Novalis, several booklets by S. Baring Gould and the Moorcock short stories all appeared

---

[1] Who also published Butler's *Dictionary of the Tarot* in 1975 in the US.
[2] Tony Bennett, from the Bookshops thread at www.mybrightonandhove.co.uk.

from Wales. The 'Brighton – Seattle' line that appeared on book covers then looked professionally international but the US connection was only a PO Box number for another alternative bookshop in that distant city, ID Books. Still, there remains a presentiment of anti-globalisation riots and the faint whiff of teen spirit. The books were distributed by a company called Leeds Books. Michael worked on the printing press, Malcolm worked as editor and designer, Bill was the headman – but everyone joined in with everything.

Idyllic alternative fantasies don't have to fall apart from internal pressures alone. In 1974 Leeds Books went bust, owing Unicorn £12,000. Although this was a serious blow and a lot of money back then, the group persevered.

> To recover from this we bought a van and Bill and myself went on a seven week trip around the UK, visiting all the shops that had ever purchased books from us and building up direct relationships with them. My job was then to be the travelling salesman. I would leave for a week at a time with a van full of books on various routes around the country, from Plymouth to Stirling and Aberystwyth to Norwich, visiting shops every six weeks and every three weeks in London. Often at the end of the week -I returned on a Friday- there had been new arguments and falling-outs among the others.[1]

Eventually the situation became untenable. The farming couple became increasingly unhappy with the way things were going. Bill spent more and more time in London, working on the Tarot book and his own poetry. Malcolm went back to the book trade in the capital too. With contacts and a sound distribution network already up and running from the van trips,

---

[1] Tony Bennett – personal communication, 2009.

Tony Bennett started adding his own comic books, some poetry, self-sufficiency and drug books to his repertoire and, eventually, Knockabout Comics was born: the first distributors of *Furry Freak Brothers* in the UK, promoters, publishers and supporters of a variety of excellent comic artists and writers (Savage Pencil, Hunt Emerson, Alan Moore[1]) for several decades and another company destined to have the odd brush with the law[2]. Michael was the only one of the group to remain in Wales.

Back in Brighton the Unicorn shop spluttered on until 1975. After that the western end of Gloucester Road was thoroughly remodelled and other bookshops took on Unicorn's mantle. The building is now an architect's office in bright blue and yellow but it would never be quite as bright as it had once been.

Nant Gwilw, the farmstead where the still and the printing press had churned out their respective mind-freeing products is now a ruin. The printing press itself is rumoured to have ended up somewhere in Glastonbury. Where else?

Bill Butler died on 21st October 1977 at his flat in Stanlake Road, Shepherd's Bush, London. The cause of death was "unascertained" and the Coroner recorded an Open Verdict. The day before he had just finished and delivered his final book, *The Myth of the Hero*. Many people believe his death to have been suicide. Others, who were in regular contact with him, see it otherwise. Ben Hutchinson, the book dealer who befriended Butler and leased the Unicorn shop to him, wrote an obituary for the North Laine Runner (a local community magazine) describing his death as a suicide, backed up by a separate description of Butler as "a victim of that dark xenophobic undertow [of the times] cloaked by the intoxication of street

---

[1] Tony currently publishes Alan Moore's wildly anachronistic parochial up-market fanzine *Dodgem Logic*.
[2] Knockabout went to trial in 1984 for distribution of drug-related books and comics under the Obscene Publications Act. All sounding wearisomely familiar by now? *Bumper Knockabout Trial Special*, 1984

parties and squatting groups."[1] This seems to have led many people who knew Butler in Brighton to recall his death in this particular way. There was, however, no note or specific indication of suicidal tendencies. Michael Moorcock, living in London at the same time, remembers things differently:

> Bill was a very good friend and we were in close contact during the time he was writing his book *The Myth of the Hero*. I saw him or spoke to him every day. After completing the book he was very wired and tired. He delivered the manuscript and went home. Unable to sleep, he took half a largactyl, the only 'downer' available in the house, and washed it down with some lager. Then he went to bed and began to snore heavily. The two people in the flat didn't like to disturb him, even though his state became somewhat dramatic. As a result, Bill didn't wake up again and died in the ambulance on his way to the hospital. Hardly an overdose. Actually a freak accident.[2]

Accidental death or suicide? – "Perhaps neither of these theories is true. Perhaps one or the other or both is relevant. They are given to show...the individual where he has been, where he is, where he has to go."[3]

If this episode seems to have ended where it began, in London, there remain several small but significant additions. Pete Scott, book-runner, Portslade resident and regular face at the Colin Page bookshop in Duke Street remembers visiting Collinge and Clark, booksellers of Leigh Street, London[4] and

---

[1] (Wright, 1997)
[2] 'Moorcock's Miscellany' website thread from 2007.
[3] Bill Butler theorising on the use of Tarot cards. (Butler, The Definitive Tarot, 1975)
[4] And the frontage used in *Black Books* TV series opening credits.

specialists in small private presses. They had purchased an unidentified pile of material from someone who had cleared a deserted flat some years back. It was Bill Butler's collection.

Perhaps it never ends. Still in Wales, Mike Hughes, Bill's partner, has published a collection of Butler's poetry, *Static of Star-filled Winds*, in a limited print run in 2001. His poetry was never going to set the world alight but the artist often leaves more than just his art to the future. Bill even has his own MySpace page.

```
┌─────────────────────────┐
│  SOLSTICE               │
│   BOOK                  │
│   SHOP                  │
│                         │
│   It's great to see you open
│   after these months of searching
│   for premises. As successors to
│   SYMPOSIUM and, before them,
│   UNICORN, you are sure to fill
│   a gap in all our lives. Welcome.
│         Brighton Voice Collective.
│                         │
│  28 Trafalgar St.       │
│   tel 692880.           │
└─────────────────────────┘
```

THIEVES AND POETS – Symposium and Solstice

...every generation starts from scratch...turning over the fragments of the past docs show a few possible lines of continuity...the great way of transmission would be the second hand bookshop...where the dreams of the past are sold cheap to the dreamers of the present.[1]

Clash t-shirts in Primark, William Burroughs in W.H. Smith, Ramones purses and Sex Pistols' baby-gros. Alternative to what? Underground from where? Independent of what? It is too

---

[1] (Duncan, 2008)

easy to forget that it wasn't always as simple as it appears now to get access to 'controversial' material, be it in the form of alternative culture, radical politics, independent music or freak poetry. If, in fact, such things can even be said to exist in the same way. Counter culture now advertises the polar opposite of its older meaning.

Despite the fundamental contradiction of working in shops, the hippie contingent strove to remain independent, anti-capitalist and anti-consumerist. The shops were a focus, a nexus for all manner of political and literary activity, attempting to be far more than simply a place to buy more stuff, just as Martin Parnell suggested in 1967. Meetings, readings, small presses, poetry, music, art exhibitions: all found under one roof, together with like-minded people. City Lights in San Francisco, Compendium in London, these were the examples. Nowadays probably only the Cowley Club on London Road could be seen as a similar physical space for radical politics, while Dragon's Gate in St. James Street is the only serious occult shop in town, despite what visitors may think when they wander the North Laines. And these two are only isolated fragments of a once greater underground culture.

It has become a truism to suggest that the small press (poetry, music, fanzines, politics) has been particularly affected by the rise of the internet. Radical information exchange and art outside of the mainstream used to need the physical nexus of bookshops or galleries, Arts Labs or supportive, free-thinking cafés.

The web altered that. It doesn't make the web 'alternative' or definitively underground by any means. It remains simply an unparalleled virtual space, occasionally policed but largely free (at least in the West). This lack of physical focal points may perhaps have contributed to the difficulty of defining anything to be against. Put simply, anti-capitalism is a tall order and can be an irritatingly vague ethos, swinging wildly from reductive single-issue protests (Smash EDO!) to all-embracing generalities (Stop the City![1]). If the punks didn't have to come in from the suburbs to see the Pistols, where would the confrontation appear? Now that you can order any number of alternative technology books on the net, why travel? Get your solar panels and wind turbines going, get your organic vegetables delivered to your door. Hear your own band, and any other band, on YourSpace, print *every single word* of your poetry on a website. Every pub, every café in Brighton, is happy, desperate even, to host your meetings. Everyone has access. No-one will say no. And an unanswerable question: is this better?

My apologies: I seem to have slipped off the subject somewhat.

When Unicorn left Brighton there were others more than willing to pick up the alternative baton; a legacy that was equal parts shamanic talking stick, joint and protest banner.

Brighton Books, run by the Hon. Julian Harding, an established shop in the heart of Brighton's South Lanes area at 12 Market Square[2] was closing down and the premises were up for grabs. Chris Reed, Anthony Hindson and Richard Inverarity bought up the lease and the remaining stock of both Brighton Books and some from Unicorn in February 1973. Chris had hung around at Unicorn, slightly in awe of the tall American poet who ran it, and learnt a lot from Bill Butler. Their bookshop was called

---

[1] The City managed to do a good job of that without much help, as it turns out.
[2] -"...friendly, stock intelligently chosen and arranged, comfy poufs (!) to sit on, and quick ordering service." This description from *Alternative Brighton*: the date of this Unicorn publication, 1974, seems a little late given its content and comments. Perhaps this is a more apt description of Symposium?

Symposium and, philosophical references aside, it was a name calculated to make people think that a South Coast version of Camden's magnificent Compendium bookshop had arrived. They continued Butler's successful, if legally risky, strategy of importing from the US. While Butler knew East Coast beat poets personally, Symposium dealt with important West Coast distributors, bringing in science fiction, poetry, and studies in spirituality, magic and radical politics: "Steven Gaskin, Alan Watts, Fritz Perls, Philip K. Dick. We sold Marx alongside astrological ephemeris, R. D. Laing, and Chogyam Trungpa. Of course, we refused to sell Linda Goodman's Sun Signs or anything that remotely resembled a best seller."[1] Laudable sentiments to be sure, but an indication that the 'alternative' was already beginning to be sliced-up, de-fanged and neatly re-packaged, to end up smeared thinly over a heterogeneous variety of retail outlets and ending up as the 'Mind, Body, Spirit' section[2].

Anthony Hindson left the fledgling business after a year, moving to California to study guitar and classical Indian music. Working with such jazz luminaries as Zakir Hussain, Larry Coryell and Shankar, he has gone on to become an internationally-renowned jazz musician.

Meanwhile, back in the South Laines, Chris and Richard were busy expanding the shop. The upper floor of the building was opened and part of it given over to a gallery where Sean Sprague held an early photographic exhibition. Sprague's continuing work as a photojournalist with international aid agencies, showcasing relief and development work in crisis-hit countries, certainly fits the peaceful, 'one-world' spiritual concerns of the shop at the time. So it came as an unpleasant surprise when a regular customer, a lecturer from the Polytechnic no less, was caught stealing a bag of books, something he had

---

[1] Caitriona Reed, blog article 2007.
[2] In a deeply concerned attempt to inject a little outrage and antagonism into what is now a largely meek, fluffy and untroubling market niche, a Waterstone's bookseller once suggested simply renaming the section 'Heresy'. Take that, angelology.

apparently done several times before. The business could ill afford this kind of thing, made worse by the fact that the miscreant managed to smash a plate glass window while making his escape!

Like Unicorn, Symposium tried their hand at publishing, too. A small poetry anthology called *Open Door* was published in 1974 with translations of Rene Char, Apollinaire and Rimbaud. Others poets contributing included Bill Butler, Jeremy Harding and Jeff Nuttall (Chris Reed also published a poetry collection in 1978, entitled *Twelve Poems*, through Solstice).

Once again, though, things ended on a sour note. Inverarity lost three thousand pounds on the horses: not the kind of damage a small independent bookshop can withstand (or, for that matter, the kind of thing they might expect: drug deals gone awry, public prosecutions and their day in court, demons eviscerating the staff – now that's what *should* have been happening). That was an enormous amount of money in the early seventies. The shop entered a phase where someone needed to close it to move on (Chris Reed left for India in March of 1976) while others held out (Inverarity lived in a flat above the shop and refused to budge). Chris was offered a good external deal for the whole shop -name, stock and site- but had already made a verbal agreement with Tim Pullman, Geoff Moore (who worked at Symposium) and Paul Bonnett. Therefore, in the continuing alternative tradition of putting friends and words before money, she kept to this. Eventually these three took the remaining stock and bookshelves from 12 Market Square and began a new chapter.

Solstice opened at 28 Trafalgar Street in the spring of 1977. Things had changed in Brighton and the real world by then. The punks took over from the hippies as the hippies had taken over from the beats, the mods and the rockers. And similar battles were waiting to be fought. Same as it ever was (he said, anachronistically).

Richard Branson opened a very early branch of Virgin Records at the Clock Tower in Brighton, where the giant new

Boots is now. Nobody seems entirely sure when this happened. Some claim that it may have been his first shop, opened before the Oxford Street branch (1971) while others are sure it was later, more like 1973. Virgin skipped to the other side of Queen's Road when the block and the famous Regent Cinema were demolished in 1974, then up to Western Road and into the old Boots building (which had housed a major circulating library once upon a time) before the move to its final resting place inside the new Churchill Square.

More precisely, on 27 March 1976 Dame Anita Roddick, "Entrepreneur, Retailer, Activist"[1] opened the first branch of her Body Shop in Kensington Gardens. Almost from the beginning, then, Brighton hosted two major success stories of the seventies and eighties, Virgin and the Body Shop, the two brands that straddled the alternative and the mainstream, leading the public from one to the other, Branson without compunction and Roddick with zeal.

In 1977 the North Laines and Trafalgar Street were not the haven of fashion boutiques and coffee shops they are now. The Laines were designated a conservation area in the same year that Solstice opened. This preserved a little of the old town's heritage, much of which, in the area to the north around New England Street and more centrally where the Jubilee Library now stands, had been bulldozed into a wasteland. The northern side of Trafalgar Street was largely devoid of shops, apart from The Pottery Workshop (run by Peter Stocker and only recently closed). On the south side, there was the Lord Nelson pub, Bioscope Books at no.27 and, later, the Trafalgar Bookshop at no. 44 (run by David Boland until it closed, finally, in 2005).

Incidentally, Bioscope, a specialist film bookshop, would have had a good year in 1978 as the FIAF (International Federation of Film Archives) held an important symposium in Brighton on 'Film 1900-1906'. 548 short silent films were shown in the Brighton Film Theatre, formerly and aptly, a music hall at

---

[1] According to the blue plaque on the site. It's a description that effectively sums up the contradictions of the hippy ethos.

63a North Road. International film archivists were swarming the town and the event has become an important reference point for academic studies of early film, as is fitting for one of the birthplaces of film itself[1]. The manager of Bioscope, Ross McKinnon-Chorlton also used to frequent another, older establishment: the Theatre Bookshop in New Road. Founded in 1962 by a Mrs Tee, an "amicable silver-haired lady with a slight squint"[2], this large, three storey shop catered for all theatrical tastes, selling old theatrical magazines and Victorian and Edwardian postcards as well as books. Very sensibly, it was situated in the same road as the Theatre Royal. The business was taken over in the early seventies by Mr. R. Atkinson, after Mrs. Tee's death, and finally disappeared, possibly in a move to Arundel, around 1978.

Further back in the North Laines, at Solstice on Trafalgar Street, Paul Bonnett remembers the area as "deeply unfashionable...so rents were more reasonable." Décor came in the form of fake palm trees from the Virgin in Queen's Road, which was undergoing a revamp (the 'Island Records' image probably not punk enough for them at the time) and the comfortable pouffes once again. The reading-room feel made the place an excellent hang-out and meeting-place but did little for sales in the long run.

Stock continued the Unicorn/Symposium tradition while expanding to include more science fiction and children's books. Paul says that the book that "pretty much represents our values is *The Last Whole Earth Catalog*" out of San Francisco. The *Whole Earth Catalog* was published by Stewart Brand in the US between 1968 and 1972 and then occasionally afterward until 1998. Like Unicorn's *Survival Scrapbooks*, it became an important source of information.

For this new countercultural movement, information was a precious commodity. In the

---

[1] For once, it is reasonable to add 'Hove, actually'.
[2] Bernard Dutton-Briant – mybrightonandhove website message board.

'60s, there was no Internet; no 500 cable channels. [... The WEC] was a great example of user-generated content, without advertising, before the Internet. Basically, Brand invented the blogosphere long before there was any such thing as a blog. [...] No topic was too esoteric, no degree of enthusiasm too ardent, no amateur expertise too uncertified to be included. [...] This I am sure about: it is no coincidence that the Whole Earth Catalogs disappeared as soon as the web and blogs arrived. Everything the Whole Earth Catalogs did, the web does better.

- Kevin Kelly:
The Whole Earth
September 17, 2008

Again, while true in the main, this blithely positive attitude to the web does have a tendency to overlook the individual places that stocked and distributed the physical copies of the magazines and books that the counter-cultural hungered after. The web is still not a place where you can hang out under plastic palm trees flipping through the latest import paperbacks and know that there isn't anywhere else like this in fifty miles. You are in a particularly conducive environment, a special place. And in on a secret. And that is going to produce a different kind of mind-set than popping into Borders or ordering from amazon.

Aside from poetry, mysticism, psychotherapy and the occult, Solstice had martial arts selections, underground comix (*Furry Freak Brothers* from the US via Tony Bennett and *Metal Hurlant* from France), guitar and other specialist magazines like *Asimov's Science Fiction*, *Analog*, *The Leveller*, *Co-evolution Quarterly* and *Resurgence*. American imports (from Book People distributors, based in San Francisco) included the City Lights Books catalogue and Black Sparrow Press (Charles Bukowski, Paul Bowles and the like). It was also possible to out-manoeuvre the UK market sometimes. Princeton University published Carl

Jung and their US imports were cheaper than the UK Routledge editions. And everybody read Jung then[1]. Paul says that Solstice also got hold of Frank Herbert's *Dune Messiah*, sequel to his award-winning SF novel *Dune*, before it was available in the UK. I had to travel to London (from Deepest Somerset) and negotiate the seedy back alleys of Soho to buy that kind of stuff from the vast emporium of comics and science fiction known as 'Dark They Were and Golden-Eyed'; their huge amount of stock as unwieldy as the name. And, just as 1978 was Bioscope's year, the 37th World Science Fiction Convention (Seacon) was held at the Metropole Hotel in August 1979, significantly increasing sales of SF at Solstice at least for a while. Naturally, memoirs of the convention[2] make almost no mention of the town itself, except for inevitable comments on hotel prices and the excessive number of pebbles on the beach.

If Solstice had trouble sourcing science fiction, they would recommend Vortex, a specialist SF bookshop up at Preston Circus, run by Simon de Wolf, a full-bearded Dr Who fan.

Hardcore SF fandom and radical therapies aside, Raymond Briggs' *Fungus the Bogeyman* was Solstice's all-time bestseller. The author, who worked at Brighton Art College in those days, was also a regular customer.

Tim Pullman specialised in photography so Ansel Adams, Edward Curtis and others rounded out a wide selection. Paul's interests were reflected in the Martial Arts and Eastern philosophy books (*Zen and the Art of Archery* by Herrigel, for example) while Geoff Moore provided the Astrology material for the burgeoning evening classes in the area. In 1979, Solstice and Public House Bookshop jointly organised a poetry reading by Allen Ginsberg and Peter Orlovsky at the Meeting House in the South Lanes. In September, at the beginning of each academic year, when new batches of wide-eyed students invade the town,

---

[1] In the following decade, N.F. Brookes would provide students with remaindered Freud: there's an academic paper in that shift. Somewhere.
[2] (various, Ansible 2/3 (online archive), 1979)

the shop would run bookstalls at the University of Sussex. Friendly contacts included Infinity Foods, the Pulse Wholefood café and the local Anti-Nazi League.

As ever, there were moments that highlighted less positive changes in the cultural and political climate of the late seventies.

> We used to stock Socialist Worker (the weekly paper of the SWP) which got us into serious trouble a few times. We were threatened with being bombed and set on fire on two occasions and we had our windows smashed twice. There was a third attempt when we were open on a Saturday afternoon. A drunk National Front member threw a bottle at the window but it bounced off the frame. I ran out and chased him up the road. Amazingly, a police car happened to be driving up Trafalgar Street; they got involved and we trapped the man in a car park by where GB Liners has their big store now, and he was caught. Allegedly, he was a prospective NF election candidate for Shoreham... that was the end of his political career!
> As a result of local fascist activity, we developed a close relationship with Special Branch, with 2 of them keeping a close eye on us...I am not sure they were that happy, looking after hippy booksellers, but they did their job, and were really good guys to have on your side!
>
> - Paul Bonnett

Paul, putting his interests in Martial Arts to good use, would run self-defence classes at the Resource Centre in North Road, attended by staff from Infinity Foods, local Labour activists and ANL members – "a selection of non-violent people!"

It wasn't the fascists that put an end to Solstice, though. Grinding economics did that. Paul had two children to support and alternative bookselling has never been a way to get rich. All those involved agreed to sell the shop as a going concern and in 1982 a father and son team took it over. The site was renamed Garlands Bookshop. This drifted into more second-hand territory and finally disappeared after a couple of years. Driffield, in his rabid surveys of bookshops during the eighties, could never find them open.

But Trafalgar Street could not do without books. They would be back at this location eventually. Meanwhile, however, in a street far, far away there was another alternative. Brighton's success with North American imports like Bill Butler was set to continue.

THE ESSENTIAL HERESIES
– The 70's and the Public House Bookshop

When Lee Harwood dropped off the Unicorn keys at Bill Butler's flat late in 1969, another manager was required to mind the store while Bill was off on his multifarious travels. Through arcane theatre connections, the word reached Richard Cupidi, a well-travelled North American then living in Clapham Junction. At first he thought the job was in Brixton – a positively luxurious commute. Brighton, however, is a fair bit further. But it does have an odd ability to draw people into its orbit and keep them close – unlike Bill himself unfortunately. He answered the door in a short kimono; dangerously short for a six foot man.

"Hihowareyouimfineareyougay?"

Despite such challenges to both communication and fashion, Richard did become the next manager of Unicorn. He also became an accomplished book runner, picking up hundreds of books for Unicorn and himself, selling them on to interested parties and turning a profit. He had the nose for it, as some in the trade like to say; the ability to sniff out a good book with a sense entirely unrelated to reading. This suited Bill fine. At heart, the beat poet and hippy bookstore owner was also a flagrant capitalist. This probably made it all the more galling when Richard eventually left in late 1971 to look for his own premises.

Back in 1970, the assessment of the town by the newspaper of the alternative press, *International Times*, was largely negative. The *IT* survey somehow managed to overlook Unicorn completely, despite carrying regular adverts for it in their back pages. But, as Unicorn could attest, "Brighton Council are notoriously conservative and prejudiced". And it seems that they had a lot to contend with. A 'PROBE' feature page in the *Evening Argus* from April 5th 1971[1] brought to light the no doubt terrifying fact that "Brighton has become the national headquarters of a highly-organised group of extreme Left Wing political agitators," based in Coombe Terrace off the Lewes Road in a bookshop called Progressive Books and Periodicals Ltd. The *Argus* chose to demonise and expose the Left and the alternative alike and it took a smaller, more radical local paper, to balance the books.

But, like Molotov cocktails, things could flare up and burn out too. The Brighton Combination, an 'Arts Lab' based off West Street and only the second to be established in the country, had closed after 20 months work: not through lack of support but from lack of funds and that self-destructive impulse that seems to afflict groups of apparently like-minded people as they grow bigger. Significant contributors from here moved up to the Big City and went on to establish the future success of the Deptford Albany theatre in London. Closer to the political arena, the Brighton Anarchists were disbanding. They had been agitating for some time in Brighton, producing short lived magazines like *Fleabite*, *Big Flame* and *Gutter Press*. Jim Duke, the bald, bearded, dada poet and regular contributor to *The Brighton*

---

[1] "Mao lurks in Brighton shop" – I'm surprised at the restraint in not finishing that headline with an exclamation mark.

Head and Freak Mag had moved back to his native Australia. David Lepper, in whose house the anarchists met on a regular basis, was thinking of more conventional politics[1] and John Upton's Unicorn mural was starting to flake.

On the other hand, in March 1973 a poor quality, small circulation newspaper was published out of the 'Open Café', yet another anarchist, whole-food café on Victoria Road. This went on to become the longest running alternative newspaper in England. The *Brighton Voice*, run by a collective with largely anarchist and/or socialist principles, ran for 132 issues until July 1989 and, on the way, successfully prodded the irritable town council over any number of issues. Planning permissions and the state of rented housing (the activities of slum landlord Nicholas Hoogstraten especially) were favoured bugbears. Though the *Voice* never had an enviable circulation, it was extremely popular locally, particularly with the politically active students at Sussex University. Lord Steve Bassam, Chief Whip of the House of Lords in 2008, was once a member of the *Voice* publishing collective, sitting in the Open Café, putting the world to rights, as so many still do in such persistent Brighton surroundings.

And on the retail side, too, things began to come together. Ananda, part of the coterie of 'hippie' shops, opened in Gloucester Road in 1972. Infinity Foods had been going strong since 1971. The Whole Earth Festivals on the Sussex University campus began. Certain aspects of sixties counter-culture were bedding-in and flourishing, preparing the ground for Anita Roddick and Richard Branson.

But before that, and like so many Brighton adventures, this one was built with driftwood and volunteers.

By the spring of 1973, Richard Cupidi had finally found his ideal property: 21 Little Preston Street. Not everyone would agree with this utopian assessment. Little Preston Street is not a busy thoroughfare. Despite being embedded in the Regency Square Conservation Area, with all its associated

---

[1] He later became Labour MP for Brighton Pavilion in 1997.

splendour, it is in fact the backside of the numerous restaurants which front on its bigger brother, Preston Street. It's where the deliveries come in and the rubbish waits. It's only about ten feet wide in places. Cars don't like it. Seagulls do. There are no shops or businesses along its entire length. So number 21, in 1973, was not, in modern parlance, a prime retail location. What it was was an old traditional pub, the Dependant, which had been converted into a corkscrew factory for a few years and then left derelict for several more. Outside it had no need to be boarded up as it was inches deep in posters, a palimpsest history of Brighton performances. Rusted barbed wire added to the ambience. Inside there had been a fire once. The roof was damaged. The first floor was a sooty puddle. There were abandoned workbenches, a basement and a lift.

It was fantastic.

He told the estate agents that he wanted to view 21 Little Preston Street. The man at the office looked faintly stunned to begin with, but then, after taking some time to find an ancient key on a large wooden key fob, he put his arm around this surely insane cousin from across the water who obviously had no idea what he was doing, pressed the wood and iron into his hand and said: "Take as much time as you like, old chap." That was it. Everything was set.

Richard's flatmate, Maurice, ran the Smallest Theatre in the World: a tent erected from a motorcycle sidecar. He would drive around and do shows anywhere. They effectively squatted no.21 and began to do it up. With friends, carpenters and volunteers, the building grew into something new and unusual. Anything that came to hand could be incorporated. A porthole from a ship was found and sunk into the trap door of the beer barrel chute, opening up the basement to sunlight that it had never have seen before. Floors were repaired and the roof went back to doing its proper job. The traditional pub exterior with its curved glass and panelled wood was cleaned up and retained, but above this, artist Neal Dean painted an alchemical mural: a bearded ancient thinker in the sky, pointing out the stars in a book with a motto from Ezra Pound: "The book should be a ball of light in your hands"

Eventually officialdom had to be addressed but this turned out to be almost as easy as getting the key. Over the phone and with no negotiation, Richard got a seven year lease and three months rent free –for doing the place up- from the landlord.

There was one other piece of luck. At the bottom of a chest of books sold to Richard as a job lot were two books. Rebound in the nineteenth century, they were the collections of an Italian poet, printed in Venice in 1601. As it turned out, one of them was a unique copy. Not only that but the father of one of Richard's friends was a University professor whose particular obsession was that very Italian poet. Public House cost around £900 to set up. Two thirds of the money came from the sale of that one book. A little poetry goes a long way sometimes. Even in Brighton.

In 1973 the bookshop competition for Public House was reasonably high. In town were Bredon's and Beal's in East Street, Robinson's in Meeting House Lane, the recent Quadrant in Imperial Arcade, Brighton Books in Market Street with Combridge's and Practical Books out towards Hove. Almost all of these had second-hand departments. Quadrant's old branch was at 12a Queen's Road, later the first home of Noel Brookes' shop. Holleyman & Treacher and George Sexton were the old-timers with Ben Hutchinson in Trafalgar Street, Kenny Lane in Blatchington Road and Rowan-Robinson in Montpelier Road. There was the three-storey Theatre Bookshop in New Road, the cheap paperbacks of Studio 4 in Little Western Street, the "stimulating" magazine collections of Two-Way Books in Gardner Street (which is still there!) and Bioscope for film books. And Unicorn was still hanging on.

Public House, though, as it publicly proclaimed, wanted to be "not just a bookshop".

There was competition of a decidedly more aggressive sort throughout the seventies. Solstice on Trafalgar Street was not the first, nor by any means the last, to encounter thuggery and trouble. It might come as a surprise to the more modern entrepreneurial capitalist of Brighton, more than willing to welcome all races, creeds and orientations (with money) with open arms, that the town has often shown a far less convivial side in the past. It begins conservatively, continues through Conservatives and descends steeply into the stygian depths of far-right fascism. From Oswald Moseley's training/holiday camps on the South East coast in the 1930s via the violence of Mods and Rockers to the petty, vindictive provincialism that characterised the Unicorn court case, Brighton has always walked a fine line between radical openness and offended prejudice, between alternative and traditional, between, in this particular decade, left and right.

The National Front and its associated local splinter groups were the bane of left-inclined (socialist, communist, trade unionist, anti-nuclear) or aging hippy anarchist co-ops all over the UK. The NF's local action groups were all named to bring to mind some terrifying Nazi strike force; in fact they were far more likely to be drunken thugs goaded into half-assed 'plans' by individuals in pubs happy to provide racists and virulent nationalists with a little drinking space. And sometimes even a disco.

Within a year of opening, Public House had been firebombed. After dark and ineffectively, of course. On the night of April 7th 1973, a home-made incendiary device was pushed through the letter box of the shop. Luckily it landed in such a way that the firework fuse burnt against the sturdy wooden door and eventually went out, failing to properly ignite. The mark stayed on the door for many years: a sign of the times.

The attack was reported in the second issue of the new radical paper, the *Brighton Voice*: 'Anarchists foil bomb plot'. The police, after about forty of them had turned up and taken a disingenuous interest in the VD handbook, were unhelpful and the investigation quickly reached a 'dead-end'. But the report in the *Voice* does provide an early description of the shop and its guiding principles, to which it remained true for almost a quarter of a century.

> The Public House is a non-profit bookshop, founded upon concepts of mutual aid and direct involvement in the community; we also provide a free anarchist library, community printing service and try to keep information and a bit of joy circulating. We don't go in for heavy image-mongering...[1]

The shop could be all things to all men and women. Alongside Richard Cupidi, John Kieffer had a particular interest in new music, free and avant-garde jazz. The shop stocked a striking selection of imported vinyl bootlegs and was one of the first in the country to promote the Eurocentric jazz label ECM, established in 1969. Anyone who worked there could use the shop as a base of operations for whatever wild concept seized their imaginations. Richard points to the history of the basement alone as an indication of the dizzying array of projects that came and went. The low-ceilinged single room that was once choked with barrels of traditional English ale first housed a printing press (that produced both *Attila* and the *Brighton Voice* in its day), worked as an alternative medicine room for massage and meditation, saw any number of band rehearsals, served as a poetry and music performance space, was a catalogue and mail order workshop, an arts and crafts workshop, a trading post and a gallery. Its main and relatively constant use was simply as a collective meeting space for the shop. Static black and white photos from the time belie this considerable industry. Instead, relaxed indeterminate figures lie around in a more conducive smoky haze than the fascists firebomb produced.

To celebrate their first year, Richard baked a cake. A psilocybin birthday cake. Along with a fine line in home-made

---

[1] ('M.B', 1973)

salsa, it was the start of something good that would last over twenty five years.

From the days of the Beats and then Unicorn, Allen Ginsberg and his partner Peter Orlovsky came over from the US to read poetry and cast an appreciative eye over the premises. The Beat-father proclaimed the tiny, out-of-the-way shop "better than City Lights" and improvised two blues poems as tribute. Richard helped to found the Radical Books Federation, a network of publishers, promoters and booksellers, and another means of fostering contact, communication and that all-important joy that was a motivating force from the beginning.

The annual Brighton Festival began in 1966 but the spin-off, more 'alternative' collection of events known as the Fringe, was only properly organised in 1993. Before that things were arranged independently and Public House promoted the precursors and inspiration for the Fringe. Free events, exhibitions, workshops and performances were given by many people who have since become rather more famous than they were when they played or performed in the Public House basement and at other venues around town. The 'Extended Series' which ran from May 8th to June 17th in 1978 saw poetry performances from Bob Cobbing (that old performance poet compatriot of Bill Butler's), Eric Mottram, Stefan Themerson, Lee Harwood and Iain Sinclair, music from Evan Parker, Barry Guy, Steve Beresford, Paul Rutherford and David Toop, and exhibitions by Toop and John Upton of Unicorn fame. Richard lectured on the Shaker movement in America while John Kieffer talked about Improvised Music. An Indian Banquet was held in the suitably exotic Hanbury Arms and an Independent Book Fair took place with stalls and readings at the Resource Centre.

By 1979 the Festival had grown even further with a proper Committee and a variety of funding from the Arts Council and the South East Arts Association. There were more venues and more participants; Keith Tippett, Viv Stanshall, Louis Moholo and Ivor Cutler were all in town.

The dark side was still making its presence felt though. In the late seventies there was a polar opposite to the Public House press and meeting place on the other side of town. In a letter printed in *Brighton Voice* 41 (1977), Tory MP Andrew Bowden reveals a National Front "secret printing press at Sutherland Road". The workshop belonged to Allen Hancock (an "old Moseleyite") and his wife (a "racist german"), NF members who also owned the notorious "Whites Only" Heidelberg Hotel in Rock Gardens. Their son, Anthony, ran the press that produced such heinous trash as "Did Six Million Really Die?" and other greatest hits of the far-right. Bill Smith, now of *Latest* magazine and back then playing in a punk band heavily involved with the Troops Out of Ireland movement, remembers violent encounters. There was a rehearsal space in a basement at the bottom of Rock Gardens and street trouble was a regular occurrence in the area. Clashes between groups were common but not likely to get reported to the authorities by either side. Single attacks and property damage did at least show up in the ever-vigilant *Brighton Voice*. Amidst all the vigorous questions and sarcasm around the contemporary issues of social security, squatting, feminism, CND, Ireland and the local press, the *Voice* kept a close eye on the far right.

In 1979, a shop assistant at Simple Supplies Wholefood shop was beaten up by 'youths' who went on to smash the door frame and throw a bottle at the windows of the Solstice bookshop in Trafalgar Street. The windows didn't break this time, but they had been broken five times in the previous eighteen months. The NF were almost certainly behind the fire which destroyed the Resource Centre in 1981. No wonder both Richard Cupidi and Paul Bonnett added self-defence courses to the already wide repertoires of their respective bookshops.

The Front made one further attempt to burn Public House. But more unpleasantly (and, Richard admits, to slightly more effect), a group of men wandered into the shop one day and physically attacked him while trying to trash the place. Narrowly avoiding having a metal fire extinguisher unexpectedly thrown at one's head is not pleasant. The shop was a small place and the desk and cash register only provide so much defence. Luckily a customer on his way out heard and saw the attack and did the best thing possible under the circumstances: ran out into the street shouting that he would fetch the police. After giving no indication of backing down and every indication of fighting back, Richard got the men out of the shop, also successfully preventing them from throwing a bench through the windows before they left. After that, no-one worked there alone.

When a National Front march was planned through Brighton, these events prompted Richard to call in some favours. On the day of the march, the Public House Bookshop played host to at least a dozen local bus drivers, big men walking with ominously straight legs, slightly bemused at the variety of literature on offer. Once again, the *Brighton Voice* had been reporting and supporting the Bus Unions in their opposition to the one-man-one-bus moves that would result in job losses and safety issues for drivers. Nothing happened that day. No-one came near the shop. It is even possible that genuine customers may have been a little intimidated by large lefty bus drivers tooled up for a fight.

Public House was not often quiet, though. Outlasting the alternatives of Symposium and Solstice, the politics of the Odd Volume and the short-lived sorceries of Grimoire and Avalon Books, the shop worked in concert with the local Resource Centre and a variety of venues, to create opportunities galore. A Women's Bookweek and related events were proposed, advertised and successfully held in 1984: "...the collective is now winding down from the week and wondering where to go next[1]" There were 'Lost Weekends' when visiting speakers held forth on eclectic subjects: Eric Mottram was back at the cutting edge, talking about poetic form and that "new alchemist", the computer. There were talks on nineteenth-century communes, radical papers and early co-ops, quickly followed by silliness: "an endless spoof adventure story" night with Paul Evans, "poet and

---

[1] From an advert in the *Brighton Voice*.

leprechaun". Graham Ackroyd, father of novelist Peter, would drop in to chat about poetry.

As far as the nuts and bolts of a business were concerned, the books and magazines in the shop remained the finest selection outside London. The ordering sessions, involving all members of staff and fuelled by fiery salsa, were a whirlwind of obscure publishers' catalogues and fiercely-defended decisions. Just when UK students were discovering the difficult delights of deconstruction and celebrating the Death of the Author, Public House was where you could find all the right words. Translated from French and imported from the States, this was where Derrida, Lacan, Deleuze and Guattari, *Radical Philosophy* and the semio-texte volumes were to be found. Poetry, tarot cards and all the major reading lists from the wiser Sussex University lecturers were on the shelves. And when you had gleaned all you needed to know about the law of the margins or the mirror stage, or you had simply given up, the ragged tomes could always be sold to the Odd Volume near the station for kindred souls to repossess.

Public House also became famous for a particular and abiding interest of Richard Cupidi's: Native American cultures and story-telling. Many people had their first introduction to this via a visit to Public House. The basement was turned into a Trading Post for Native American Arts and Crafts and banquets were held where Richard and volunteers were ably assisted by Ray Mears, already testing his ability to eat anything under the sun. A charity, the Native American Indian Trust, was set up and run from the shop for a number of years.

All good things come to an end. Ever the exception to a general rule, Public House went with good grace and a degree of calm into the endless night. Following the demise of the Net Book Agreement in the early nineties, and the slow but inexorable rise of the internet, sales and profits were inevitably squeezed. Recognising this, Richard gave the shop and the staff a year to try as many options as possible in an effort to circumvent what now seems inevitable. Nothing, though, was quite enough. In the end the shop was effectively run down in the space of a year. True to form, the smallest creditors were paid off first. The local magazines and independent distributors, always on a financial knife-edge, got their money. The bigger companies could wait. It is important to point out that this is the complete opposite of what happens when a large company goes into liquidation or administration. As one customer among many, if you have a £10 voucher from a dissolving company or have a self-produced offering somewhere in the shop, you're not likely to see that money, and probably not the stock, ever again. CEOs, Managing Directors and landlords will certainly be paid, though.

Last orders at Public House were called in 1999 and, for a while, the building reverted to dereliction. Now, as if time were moving backward there, the Dependant public house is visible once more but the 'ball of light' mural is extinguished.

A ROARING BARGAIN
- The Odd Volume, Tall Storeys and Picture Books

> Book Collecting, I would have you know, is a full-time occupation, and one wouldn't get far if one took time off for frivolities like reading.
>
> - A.N.L.Munby
> King's College Librarian, Cambridge

On the top floor of the Jubilee Library, the Rare Books Store houses over 45,000 volumes donated over the years by collectors and eminent men of the town. In a carefully-controlled environment, vast white armoires glide noiselessly at the touch of three-handled wheels, opening up vistas of huge leather folios, Victorian children's books, manuscript histories of

Brighthelmston, yards of 'Philosophical Transactions' and boxes of intriguing miscellaneous pamphlets. Somewhere in there is a tiny quarto entitled Cruickshank's *The Odd Volume*. Next to the store, in the reading room, is a plaque to the man responsible for this quiet resource, Tony Miller.

Like so many significant inhabitants of Brighton, Tony Miller was not born here. A Lancashire lad from St. Helen's, he left for University at Imperial College London and then onto a degree in Social Psychology at Sussex University between 1973 and 1976. He returned to London for a Cultural Studies MA at Chelsea College and there he fell in with a rum crowd. Among the tat and antiques of Portobello Road, Tony and two student friends from Sussex, David Brewer and John Dodds, ran a shop and stall with author and journalist Iain Sinclair and the incomparable Driffield. It is easy to imagine them caught up in the mutable fiction surrounding Sinclair's tales of book dealers and poets[1], which he must have been writing at the time, and Driffield's later scathing assessments of the entire country's second-hand bookshops. The trio of friends eventually bought a sizeable quantity of no doubt impeccable quality stock from Driffield, shut up shop, ducked out of London and succumbed to the inevitable.

The call of the South Coast got to them in the end. In 1979, Brewer, Dodds and Miller returned to Brighton to set up The Odd Volume bookshop at 53 Upper Gloucester Road, just down from the station. The site has been completely redeveloped now and there is no longer any sign of their small shop or of the umbrella and bag emporium next door. The trio bought their shop fittings – or more accurately, some planks – from another book shop that was on the move. Picture Books, established at 91 Dyke Road in 1977 by Camilla Francombe and Stuart Broad, was relocating to larger premises at 88 St James' Street. In this theatrical and eccentric part of an eccentric town, the previous occupant of the top flat, a dancer, would winch her lover up through the top window when he wanted to visit. Laurence

---

[1] (Sinclair, 1987)

Olivier would pop in from his home in Royal Crescent on the sea front. Camilla saw off the redoubtable George Holleyman when it came time for Olivier to sell off some of his collection of theatre books.

The two shops remained connected in later years as well. David Brewer left the Odd Volume for other pastures in 1983 while John and Tony eventually bought out Camilla and Stuart in St James' Street and renamed that shop Tall Storeys. When Tony joined the Council, John ran this alone for a while and even opened a Tall Storeys Too branch in the increasingly fashionable Kensington Gardens before selling on once again. These new owners created the locked upstairs room that I so diligently explored despite having no money. Camilla went on to run a vast eponymous cathedral of books in Eastbourne, while her mother, Kim Francombe, had been doing the same in Worthing since 1971. In more recent times, Kim's, run by Lin Flowers, closed but two other branches are now in Arundel and Chichester and "in capable hands".

Back in Brighton, and unusually for a bookshop owner, Tony was both a reader and a collector. His collection of twentieth-century first editions was second to none and, what's more, he had actually read almost every book in the shop. He was also a staunch Labour supporter. By the mid-eighties, Driffield, their old cohort, was his usual sniffy self about distractions from the business of books, such as politics or actual reading. He certainly seemed to prefer the new Picture Books, describing it in unusually glowing terms as "by far the best shop in Brighton" in his first guide. Tony Miller probably didn't much care at that point. He was too interested in what could be done in the wider world to be concerned about such sarcastic taunts:

> The new style young booksellers Mark II, University educated, left wing, written one unpublished novel and too dim to live on

social security. The name of this shop refers to the number of books they sell.[1]

Driffield doesn't give us a fair or interesting review entry because i) we don't insult him enough, ii) we've no books under 50p, in bad condition, piled up on the floor, iii) our shop has proper lighting & heating and full shelves in alphabetical order, iv) he's never managed to make off with a roaring bargain...[2]

The Odd Volume was a fine shop, a haven for University students on the lookout for cheap text books that had already done the rounds of the Falmer campus once or twice. There was an almost visible flow of certain books round here. From Noel Brookes' shop in Queen's Road just down the hill, new Shakespeares and Freuds would get pencil annotations on their way out to the University campus and then be returned to the Odd Volume at the end of term only to be snapped up by the next batch of students and start the trip again, becoming increasingly worn and marked in the process.

But there was more to do than simply run a bookshop. Bill Smith was in a local political punk band called the Alternative British Army and, when they met at the shop soon after it opened, Tony soon became their manager. They became good friends, and Tony managed several successive incarnations of the band including their more famous turn as Rhythm Tendency. Between them, Bill and Tony took on and promoted a number of successful bands and comedy acts in eighties Brighton. There was regular comedy and cabaret at the Richmond and Thomas Mapfumo playing in a fish and chip restaurant on the Pier.

Apparently even this wasn't enough. Sitting in the Volunteer pub (now the Mash Tun on New Road), Tony sat with

---

[1] (driff, 1985)
[2] From the Odd Volume advert in driff, directly opposite the first quote.

Bill, Richard Paul Jones, the late writer and broadcaster Pete McCarthy and Neil Butler, founder of the Zap Club on the seafront, to hammer out some ideas as the drink flowed. Between them, they decided that Brighton, with all its activities, events and socialising, needed a proper listings magazine - especially as most of those bands and comedians were being promoted by the very same people then sitting around the table. And the *Punter* was born.

Tony was, according to Bill Smith, "a natural press guy...a skilled designer, writer and networker, before the word was even invented". The *Punter* was a highly successful magazine, running from 1984 to 1997 and originally featuring such luminaries as Julie Burchill, Chris Eubank, Mark Kermode, Jon Ronson and Jonathan Ross. Dominy Hamilton, daughter of the famous post-war Pop artist Richard Hamilton, worked at the Odd Volume for a spell. She re-worked her father's most famous collage -'Just what is it that makes today's homes so different, so appealing?' -for the cover of the March 1987 issue. Taking his cue, perhaps, Bill Smith now runs the *Latest Homes* stable of magazines and websites which still include event listings amongst the myriad of Estate Agents.

Tony and Bill promoted the Real Sounds of Africa musical troupe in 1987. They bought two buses, rented a house, brought the band over and toured the country. It was fun. And successful in its way. But it wasn't lucrative. The music scene wasn't quite ready for that level of variety yet. They preceded the World Music boom by too many years. And they lost about a hundred grand in the end.

Tony thought it was time to get a proper job. In 1989 he moved into local politics for good. He had already run Steve Bassam's (now Lord Bassam) unsuccessful Parliamentary campaign in 1987 and had many friends and connections with the local Labour Party and the town council. With his background it was only natural that he should begin a new career as a press officer.

At this point the final issue of the *Brighton Voice*, still wishing to appear oppositional and challenging, summed up

Tony and Bill's achievements by calling them the 'Arts Mafia'. With the acquisition of a variety of fulsome grants, the setting up of Artists Unlimited and their apparent monopoly on the running of the Council's Arts Unit, the *Voice* tried to give the *Punter* and its cohorts a bad review. They couldn't pull it off. The gigs, events and high profile of Brighton on the music and comedy scene during the eighties spoke for itself. In the end, the article could only blame the town councillors for handing out cash indiscriminately. Then the Voice went quiet and the *Punter*, and the punters, went on to enjoy themselves regardless.

Before his untimely death in 2007, Tony Miller had become Chief Executive and Director of Cultural Services and the driving force behind the new Jubilee Library. His lifelong interest in books and culture led to the establishment of an award-winning building, the reinvigoration of a derelict central town site and the creation of an ideal home for Brighton's eclectic collections of Rare Books, including *The Odd Volume*.

GIN AND ASHES - Bredons, Beals and Combridges

> Thank you again for the beautiful book, I shall try very hard not to get gin and ashes all over it, it's really much too fine for the likes of me.
>
> - Helene Hanff, 84 *Charing Cross Road*, 1970

No discounted books, cookery books with more words than pictures, autobiographies by adults of standing and reputation, subscriptions, hardbacks. Labelled sections by publisher: Pan, Fontana, Penguin... A bookshop where the only revolution was the paperback revolution and that was a long time coming. Ah, the good old days.

Despite a reputation that Brighton is now quite happy to capitalise upon, the wider and more complete picture of bookselling here is not simply tales of intellectual poets challenging the establishment and gay pride on pink streets. There was a time when traditional book retailing was not devalued and floundering, as is arguably the case today. Establishments of quality existed, and if Unicorn and their ilk wished to offer an alternative that was their prerogative, but it was of little concern to tried, trusted and, yes, more dignified emporia: the alternative to the alternative.

John Beal had been a bookbinder, bookseller and map printer in Brighton at 55 East Street since 1866. John's son, Ernest Frederick Beal (1885 - 1918) was killed in WWI and awarded the Victoria Cross after single-handedly taking out four German machine gun posts, then rescuing a wounded man from no-man's-land. He was killed by a shell the following morning. Brighton named a bus after him. John Beal & Son as a business lasted until 1968 and had expanded to numbers 56 and 52a in the same street. Despite a productive and illustrious history, they were considered mere stationers by staff at K. J. Bredon's, who bought them out in the end. George Beal, another member of the family, had a business at 207 Western Road as "printer, bookseller and stationer". In 1876 he published the *Catalogue of the Cases of Birds in the Dyke Road Museum, Brighton* by E.T. Booth, the bird-hunter and collector whose taxidermied conquests can still delight and horrify visitors in the same museum, now named after him.

Combridge's Library (later just Combridge's) began in 1901 at 56 Church Road in Hove and lasted into the 1970s, selling sheet music and records as well as books. They had a second-hand department run by Kenny Lane but in 1960 he left to run his own shop, specialising in circus books, from 52 Blatchington Road, Hove. If you can still find dilapidated paperbacks with '6d' scrawled all over the cover, that's where they are from[1]. The front of Lane's shop was stacked with awful romantic fiction, Mills & Boon for the local ladies, and he hated everything about it. His choice stock and the circus books he treasured were, in the great tradition of grumpy book sellers, out the back. Lane was another Brighton bookman who had met Aleister Crowley in later years. The magician apparently admitted

---

[1] Much like David Paine's 10p marks which ruined many a paperback on Sydney Street in the late eighties.

to some interest in circuses and their history; not something that crops up in his many biographies.

A latecomer in 1959, Robinson's Bookshop at 51 Meeting House Lane just managed to survive into the 1970s as well. But the largest and most successful bookshop of this kind emerged, with all the appearance of bad timing, just before the Second World War.

In 1962 K. J. Bredon's Bookshop at 10 East Street published a small booklet to celebrate their 25th anniversary. This cheerful and self-deprecatory little work charts their unassuming rise, with both setbacks and successes, in the years since 1937. The company, even then, felt the need to describe themselves as "new boys" in comparison with Brighton's more established businesses.

It all starts with one Kenneth Rosenthal changing his name to Bredon in order to avoid anti-Semitic feeling. At school he had been a friend of the poet W.H. Auden, and they appeared together in *The Tempest* one year. This was an early intimation of Kenneth's association with theatre celebrities that enhanced the reputation of his future shop. Later, he survived Cambridge but left without a degree.

Meanwhile, in 1931, Frederick J. Ward opened what he called 'the first modern bookshop' at 3 Baker Street in London[1]. Reacting against the traditional dark and musty, quiet-library-style shop, the venture had light, accessible shelves and front windows that did not hide the shop inside behind piles of dark tomes. The concept was a success, and has become the tradition of today, in fact; thus, in 1937, Ward decided to open a new shop in Brighton and, with the 30 year-old Kenneth as partner and a tiny staff, they took over 10 East Street. With limited space, dodgy drains, dry rot and a delayed opening, it was not an auspicious beginning. For the first two years they ran at a loss. Then, just to make things really difficult, the war happened; priorities changed and Directors and staff moved to assist the war effort.

---

[1] (Norrie, 1982) - p76

Indirectly, however, this may have helped the shop to survive. The original London branch closed down, allowing the Brighton store to become the headquarters of the company and a distribution centre for the Ward Gallery Greeting Cards. London, suffering under the Blitz, lost large chunks of the publishing industry to German bombing. Paternoster Row, the home of at least three major publishers, was completely destroyed. Some never recovered from the loss of their stocks and offices: "...the hub of the English book trade lies in smoking ruins."[1]

Suddenly, books were in short supply and surviving stockists experienced a significant increase in demand. Brighton's proximity to London paid dividends when regular visits were made to the stricken capital in order to get any books that were still available. The manager of 10 East Street returned "begrimed but triumphant, knowing the shelves would be filled for another few weeks."[2]

The popular stock of that time is itself indicative of a bygone age. Bredon's had waiting lists for traditional gems such as *English Social History*, *The Concise Oxford Dictionary* and, ironically, *War and Peace*.

The lack of books prompted further developments. A 'haphazard' second-hand department was started, as well as a technical section and a much-needed expansion into the adjoining shop became necessary.

Bredon had been working at the Ministry of Information, promoting patriotism alongside Laurie Lee and Cecil Day Lewis. When the war was over, he and Frank Ward returned to the Brighton premises. They made Margot Heginbotham (now Mrs Tyrie), who had managed the business from the start and through the difficult war years, a Director. Now was the time to get properly organised. The formidable Thora Orchard had run a hand-weaving shop in Ditchling before the war but now, returning from the Land Army, took over the

---

[1] (Norrie, 1982) - p87
[2] (unknown, 25 Years of K. J. Bredon's, 1962)

Technical Department and moved into a flat above the shop. Grace Pullinger expertly expanded the Art Department. When he left the RAF after the War, Bredon and Ward also took on Raymond Smith to run the growing second-hand and antiquarian department. His "stubborn refusal to consider any new book worthy of his attention" would make him a character not to be forgotten in years to come.

In 1946 more expansion allowed for the opening of a picture framing workshop at the rear of the shop, on the premises of what had once been the workplace of a famous local craftsman, 'Old Andrew', the net-maker. In 1947 Frank Ward sold the Brighton business to his two co-directors, moving back to London and a new shop at 124 King's Road, Chelsea. By 1956 Raymond Smith and his precious antiquarian domain had moved to 22 Prince Albert Street. Opposite him, at 2 Prince Albert Street was the equally successful Picture Department, run by Kenneth's son, Mark. By 1962 Bredon's was a major family business in Brighton, employing thirty-five staff over three large sites.

Some staff were a little in awe of the Book Department. What had been modern and challenging in Fred Ward's day quickly became staid and not a little inflexible. Alan Nelhams[1] answered an advert in *The Bookseller* while living in Edgware early in 1963. He was interviewed by Kenneth himself and started work under Miss Orchard on a month's trial. He remembers the stock as "a broad, intelligent range, but not too adventurous" and that Bredon and Miss Orchard did practically all the buying, without recourse to staff knowledge or even customer suggestions.[2] This chimes with other assessments: "[Bredon & Heginbotham's] was not a great favourite with many

---

[1] We have Alan to thank for the magnificent Edgar Brandt metal relief panels on show in Brighton. After leaving Bredon's he worked in the Clock Department at Selfridges where he noticed that the old lifts were to be replaced and their beautiful internal decoration broken up. Through numerous contacts he eventually got the destruction stopped and they were purchased by Brighton Museum.

[2] Personal communication.

representatives of publishers because Kenneth Bredon was an astute buyer who took few risks."[1] Perhaps this is precisely the kind of bookshop that Martin Parnell had in mind when he castigated the trade for reinforcing "an obnoxious form of censorship" in 1967.[2] I doubt there were many books or customers that frequented both Bredon's and Unicorn. Alan remembers an entire shelf of Loeb Library books[3] at Bredon's when he started work there. They never sold.

Visiting stage and screen actors and actresses seem to have had a liking for both Kenneth and his shops. Laurence Olivier (a one-time Brighton resident anyway), John Gielgud, Ralph Richardson, Dame Anna Neagle and Alec Guinness all liked to drop in when shows brought them to the Theatre Royal. Michael Crawford and the first Dr Who, William Hartnell, also put in appearances. Both Janet Wells, daughter of actress Susannah York, and Peter Ustinov's daughter, Tamsin, worked at Bredon's for a short time. Kenneth Bredon had local concerns too. He was made Honorary Life President of the Brighton Philharmonic Orchestra and became Chairman of the Regency Society, helping to preserve much of the town's heritage.

Raymond Smith left the business in 1963 after failing to talk the protective Kenneth into a partnership. He moved to Eastbourne and started his own antiquarian bookshop on premises that had been trading as a bookshop since 1907. Unsurprisingly, his elegant and 'good-looking' shop there bore a close resemblance to the second-hand department he had developed so effectively in Prince Albert Street. Miss Nora Ayling, who started in the book trade in 1926, took over his role at Bredon's and was still there in 1975, climbing ladders and generally putting younger booksellers to shame[4].

---

[1] (Norrie, 1982) - p203
[2] See 'The Filth – Bill Butler and the Unicorn Bookshop'.
[3] A definitive hardcover collection of classical Greek and Latin literature in bilingual translation, still available today, if you can find them.
[4] (Lewis, The Book Browser's Guide: Britain's Secondhand and Antiquarian Bookshops, 1975)

According to his son Mark, Kenneth Bredon never made much money out of his business. He was never forced to choose between books and stationery when specialisation would have made more commercial sense and he was more than happy to keep a large and cheerful staff on hand in spite of costs. He retired in 1976 and sold the business to the Hastings-based company Sussex Stationers. He died in 1997 from pneumonia brought on by a fall, aged ninety.

> Whether books are bound in paper or cloth, whether they are illustrated or not, whether the dust wrapper is plain or coloured, the bookseller is, and should be, the last link in that long chain which unites author and reader. He exists to bring them together for the benefit of each other – and that is what we have always tried to do.[1]

Keeping Bredon's name above their doors, and under the guidance of Managing Director Michael Chowen, Sussex Stationers expanded rapidly all along the South East coast. Showing belligerent but consistent vigilance, the *Brighton Voice* complained of a 'Stationery Plague' sweeping the South Coast: "Expanding out of Hastings and initially taking over Bredons (closing the excellent bookshop) and John Beals (reducing the stock lines drastically), they moved on to Combridges in Hove (making it a pale shadow of its former self) and now Walter Gillets, the last hold out in the centre of town, has gone too." The *Voice* bemoaned the "pre-packaged items at extortionate cost" and claimed that "employees of older firms are summarily fired despite years of service." With Kenneth Bredon gone, the "new boys" had grown up. It all sounds like an old story now.

With a central warehouse in Brighton, Sussex Stationers now have more than fifty outlets. But in recent years, following the departure of Chowen, they have struggled in the

---

[1] (unknown, 25 Years of K. J. Bredon's, 1962)

harsh economic climate and a recent management buy-out of the company has yet to reverse their fortunes. They still stock plenty of cards, though, just as Fred Ward and Ken Bredon would have liked it[1].

And, like John Beal's war-hero son, the town chose to honour the shop in its own way. Kenneth Bredon is the only bookseller mentioned here to have a Brighton bus named after him. Distinguished indeed.

---

[1] Sadly, things have changed as of 2011.

OCCULT POWERS - Trafalgar Street and its Skulls

It's the part of town you go to if you want your head shrunk, or your palm read, or your destiny revealed. It's the mystic, altruistic part of town. It's where they take you by the hand, and lead you through your dreams.

- *Dirty Weekend*, Helen Zahavi 1991

Solstice's old home at 28 Trafalgar Street became a gentleman's outfitters, then the home of the Brighton Peace Centre in 1984, and, after several other incarnations, re-emerged in 1998 as Kevin Daly's Rainbow Books. The spot seems to have the arcane ability to grow books out of the very walls. Rainbow's skewed window shelves and cave-like basement certainly prove this, while a cup of tea and chat with Kevin are a welcome break for and from the increasing traffic of office workers outside.

Trafalgar Street has been fertile ground for all kinds of bookshops since the nineteenth century, whether they are well-established, short-lived and inaccessible or merely phantoms. In 1889 a Thomas Tourle was at 19 Trafalgar Street while E.J. Trill was at number 7 (and Trill & Sons at 22 Duke Street too): booksellers all. Johnson & Young were at number 79 and People's Books (prop. J. Jordan) at number 90 in 1950. Bioscope has already been mentioned. Ben Hutchinson had been at number 42 since 1961 while Sheppard's Bookshop (with a home base in Hassocks) had specialised in Naval, Military and Aviation books, both new and second-hand, at number 22 since 1956. In the early nineties Brian Banks, a renowned expert on the French Decadent novelist Joris-Karl Huysmans, lasted a whole eighteen months in the street, selling books and antiques, before disappearing to Poland as a more welcoming alternative to Brighton. Driff suggests the presence of bookshop called Blain's on the northern side of the street in 1985 but only to complain that he never found it open.

Brighton, as deeply shallow as it is casually arrogant, seems happier with trendy social excesses, like the flighty female visitors to the early Circulating Libraries, than with any serious scholarly strangeness. For all my talk of mystical Masonic growths throughout the city, that is not Brighton's favourite sorcery. The town prefers its magic theatrical: rock'n'roll, performance art, graffiti and pink feather boas: drinking, putting on a show and camping it up. It's about what you wear and where you're seen. If only by comparison, the real thing fares less well.

Though Crowley was famously cremated here in Brighton, he passed away a little further down the coast. His last words were "I am perplexed" – perhaps expressing dismay that a Great Beast of his calibre could pass into the unknown at a mere boarding house in Hastings. Other than that, strange signs of the occult seem to appear outside the Brighton area: the black dogs and UFOs of Findon, teenage Satanism in Lewes and not much else. Lewes-dwelling Druid, Philip Carr-Gomm, revels in the inspirational pagan landscape between his home town and Alfriston but draws the line at the urban sprawl of Brighton.[1] There have been rumours that a twentieth century alchemist finished up in Brighton after his laboratory in Holborn was destroyed during the war but these are unsubstantiated at best. Aficionados of the occult and book collectors do go well together however. For a short time, the witchcraft 'expert' and fake Catholic priest, Montague Summers, lived in Brighton, where he was subjected to a long-running practical joke by the American collector and book dealer, C.K. Ogden. Ogden kept his own 'house-of-books' in Brighton but he also dealt in a good many cast-offs from London auctions: fine looking but incomplete sets of calf and morocco gilt bindings. These would be boxed up and shipped down to Summers who would start unpacking with interest and excitement but end up dismayed at their lack of integrity.

Bill Butler's interest in the Tarot and the occult drew him away from his Brighton bookshop for long and awkward periods. After the seventies had produced both Symposium and Solstice, in the early eighties the North Laines continued to generate more bookshops, including two occult specialists not more than the cast of a spell apart.

However, by the time of Solstice's demise, David Boland's general shop, Trafalgar Books, was well-established at no. 44 Trafalgar Street as was the 'Brighton Bookshop and Record Exchange', now known as Wax Factor.

At the end of the street where Bill Butler and Mike Hughes used to rent their flat, David Boland opened Trafalgar Books in 1980. It became the first port of call for book-lovers down from London. At least those who chose to make a bee-line for steep and grimy Trafalgar Street, rather than heading straight for the sea. There even used to be a direct exit from the Railway station, down a wide slippery flight of stairs, past a Gentleman's Barbers (Porn for the Weekend, Sir?) and the memorably

---

[1] Philip Carr-Gomm – *The Druid Way*, Earth Quest 1993.

disgusting tiled cavern that then passed for the Gents. Horrified visitors, driven on by the rank smell of piss, could emerge under the bridge, in the dark, to look down the shabby length of Trafalgar Street.

As is so often the case, the Trafalgar Books site used to be a pub. In the 19th century it was the oddly spiritual Harmonic Tavern, then the Western Star after 1900 and a tobacconist, Whale and Co., during WWII. David ran a fascinating shop, specialising in sports, though he had a fine line in old magazines and paperback mysticism, too, perhaps a result of his close proximity to Adam Ball's shop just down the road. Even the famously churlish Driff was only mildly sarcastic about Trafalgar Books in his reviews.

Rejecting impurities, Driffield and many other researchers miss out on the experience of Wax Factor in Trafalgar Street. There is a healthy selection of books hiding behind millions of compact discs, records and tapes in the shop formerly known as the 'Brighton Book and Record Exchange'. To make things simpler, all the best stuff is in the window. But not for long.

Where once there were bookshops, there is now an endless supply of cafés with more free-trade coffee than you could ever drink. The relaxed continental atmosphere exuded from number 31 Trafalgar Street (The Laines Deli) on the corner with Kensington Place belies the earlier presence there of a thoroughly disreputable bookshop, at least in appearance. In catalogues it went by many names, all over a relatively short history: Adam Ball Antiquarian Books Ltd, Adam Ball and Catherine Walton, Déjà vu Books, the Grimoire Bookshop. My favourite, though, is in the 1985 *Yellow Pages* where, by accident or design, and perhaps as a tribute to the seafront attraction, it was described as 'Antiquarium'.

Over in Whitehawk, Adam Ball's father had run Autobooks Ltd in Bennett Road, Brighton since 1948. They specialised in motors, motoring and motor racing books, both new and second-hand. Adam had been in the antiquarian book business since 1980, originally based in London, and his interests could not have been more different.

Grimoire – to choose the most appropriate name – looked quite intimidating from the outside. Peeling green paint and a cramped interior created an atmosphere in which casual browsers could feel as if they had accidentally walked into someone's busy study. Catherine Walton, inspired by the skull on Ken Johnson's desk at Avalon Books in Gloucester Road, the other new occult bookshop, soon had a collection of occult curios scattered about the shop. They dealt in some rare and esoteric materials: tribal art and antiques added to the apparent disorder. I remember being sorely tempted by a short letter from Aleister Crowley casually pinned up in a clear plastic sleeve behind the counter. As Cowper Powys suggests, this was the kind of place where you could well find the horns of an altar to outlawed thoughts. Their catalogues showed off the stock to better effect than the shop could and eventually Walton ran a mail-order-only suppliers along similar lines. She may well have been the C. J. Walton of Renaissance Books, established at 52a North Road in 1979, specialising in poetry and history and philosophy journals. It is not a giant leap into the occult from there, especially with assistance from an expert.

And Catherine Walton appeared to have two experts on hand. The extract below is from 'Catherine Walton and Déjà vu Books' catalogue 7 from 1988 but there is no indication who wrote it.

> My sincere apologies for the recent problems regarding communication. This is due to the fact that all Déjà vu stock has now been moved to Brighton for easy access, & I am now happy and proud to announce my association with Catherine Walton & her unique bookshop in Brighton, with its fine selection of artefacts and art.

Perhaps this is Adam Ball. But then in catalogue 18, probably dated around 1991, amid the celebrations of a second shop opening at 17 High Street, Glastonbury ("Manifestation and physical phenomena can now be guaranteed at last!") and looking forward to "our complete move", the business now seems to consist of "Catherine Walton (Grimoire Books) [and] Brian Banks (Déjà vu)". That's the Huysmans expert who slipped away to Poland. In fact, the apologetic note is more likely to be by him. Adam Ball set up the shop with Catherine Walton, then Brian Banks, as Déjà vu, stepped in, upping the occult density of the stock.

Driff, in his inimitable fashion, had a run-in with the owners in 1990 when the shop went from ETGOW in his estimation of 1985, down to NETGOW (easy-to-get-on-with to NOT-easy-to-get-on-with). The reported situation may have involved non-payment of monies, the Brighton police and 'missing' books but in the end Driff was merely disappointed that they had resorted to mundane legalities and not threatened to turn him into a frog. I feel his pain: bookshops can be so disappointing.[1]

Adam Ball struggled with his family circumstances. He was apparently a gay, occult bookshop owner with a drink problem: a long way from his upbringing, in theory if not in practice. The shop only lasted from the mid-eighties until 1991. Sadly, the troubled Ball effectively drank himself to death while Walton moved to Glastonbury and into the mail-order business. It was a fine shop in its day: awkward, perhaps, and overpriced but, and there is really no substitute for this attribute, endlessly mysterious.

Meanwhile, around 1984 and only a few yards down from the old Unicorn shop but on the other side of Gloucester Road, Ken Johnson and Anne Clark opened Avalon Books. Ken had been a freelance journalist for years with several books already under his belt. He wrote the novelisation of the film

---

[1] (drif, 1991)

Zoltan – Hound of Dracula no less. On the other hand, Neville Spearman had published his important and rare study of the 20th century alchemist Fulcanelli in 1980. In here is the story of alchemist Archibald Cockren, who died in Brighton around 1950, reputedly on the verge of discovering the secret of the Philosopher's Stone. For some arcane marketing reason, the publishers suggested introducing a fictitious middle name to the work, perhaps under the impression that this would contribute to the book's sales. *The Fulcanelli Phenomenon* is, therefore, by Kenneth Rayner Johnson. He had been working in the 'Brighton Book and Record Exchange' on Trafalgar Street with Mike Astill and Al Berwick before this so he knew the area and the relevant subjects. The bookshops on Trafalgar Street have always seemed able to source occult and spiritual stock very effectively. Even David Boland's shop had a decent section of Earth Mysteries and Eastern Religion.

Just as Better Books and Compendium inspired Unicorn and Symposium, so Avalon took as its model the London occult specialist Atlantis, in Museum Street, Bloomsbury. Established in 1922, Atlantis has catered for some of the most famous occultists, magicians and alchemists in the world, having seen Crowley, Dion Fortune and the occult artist Austin Osman Spare come and go. Ken was trying for a similar "eccentric's paradise" and had taken to wearing a cape around town in an effort to look mysterious. But not so mysterious that no-one would know about the shop presumably. Bill Butler affected similar apparel, though whether this was occult pose or poetic pretension is anyone's guess.

The area outside the shop was anything but mysterious. Road works pounded away constantly as the North Laines slowly and painfully moved to save itself from dereliction and neglect. The core businesses had yet to pull together: the North Laine Traders Association was not formed until 1989 and, with notable exceptions, there was little reason to visit the run-down area of greasy spoons and ancient pubs.

Unless you wanted to see the human skull on the desk at Avalon. The shop had a fine selection of fairly hard-core occult books. Mirroring the relationship between Atlantis and that other London specialist, Watkins, in Cecil Court, Ken left the Eastern spiritualism and meditative religions to others, preferring the Western magical tradition, alchemy, poetry and a sizeable second-hand department. This was, at least by comparison with today's *Buffy* and *Harry Potter* industries, the real thing. Any books by or about Crowley, the Golden Dawn, the Ordo Templi Orientalis or Dion Fortune were guaranteed to bring in customers. The late nineteenth century's lunatic blend of cosmology and religion in the form of the black bulk of Helena Petrovna Blavatsky, founder of the Theosophical Movement, also drew customers in to peruse her mighty tome *Isis Unveiled*. He also left the majority of the antiquarian business to Adam Ball so there was surprisingly little competition between the two specialists. They even worked together on some of the more interesting house clearances.

Avalon did attract the right people. One day a note was pushed through the door asking if Ken was the author of the Fulcanelli book. It was from Simon Dwyer, the writer, editor and publisher of *Rapid Eye* magazine. Soon after starting *RE* at Poplar in London in 1979, Dwyer became a more mainstream journalist and a broadcaster for BBC Radio London. With the daily bread and butter accounted for, *RE* emerged from the punk fanzine era and moved quickly and effectively into the murky arena of industrial art and music, Genesis P. Orridge and the Temple of Psychic Youth brigade; documenting many extreme underground cultures. From 2000, Creation Press published three volumes of collected writings from the magazine, in tribute to Simon, who died from AIDS in 1997. Like *Search & Destroy* (later *Re/Search*) in the US, *Rapid Eye* had a significant impact on the alternative scene, providing a platform for reports on lifestyles, conspiracy theories and music that did not often see the light of day in the overground press. For example, issue 7/8 of "the International Manual of Substance for Illuminated Illiterates" from 1986 contains interviews with both William Burroughs and Derek Jarman, articles on video censorship, mind control and TOPY and a handy illustrated guide to penis piercings.

Simon asked Ken to contribute to RE and he responded with a variety of articles on the self-styled "King of the Witches", Alex Sanders (under a pseudonym: Sanders was notoriously sensitive), the fake Tibetan monk Lobsang Rampa, and the slightly mad adventuress, Alexandra David-Neel.

Brighton, as all residents and most visitors come to know, has a reputation for interminable and inscrutable road works. The endless noise on the road outside drove Ken to distraction. Finally, in 1987, it also drove Avalon from Gloucester Road and into the Jubilee Hall, a rather sad indoor market then, only dreaming of its final transformation into the Komedia theatre complex. Finally, no amount of interest in *An Interview with Israel Regardie* (a late associate of Crowley and expert on the Sufi) or the handsome £50 hardback *Complete Rituals of the Golden Dawn* could keep the shop going. In 1989, Ken left the book trade and made his way north.

Now, as I have opined previously, the magic has largely gone away, dissolved into Mind/Body/Spirit sections, with only Bell, Book and Candle in Gardner Street and Dragon's Gate left fighting a rear-guard action against secular indifference and spiritual candy floss.

CHAOS AND OLD NIGHT - N F Brookes

"Where are your second hand books?"
"They're all in private rooms."
"Well can I see them?"
"No. They're all locked up."
"Aren't they for sale?"
"No."

- C.S. Lewis encounters staunch opposition from a 'New & Second-hand Bookshop' in Newquay, 1927.

Parallels between the world, the library and the labyrinth have been done to death. Clichés, however, get that way for a reason: because they are resonant and effective, at least in the beginning. But if our libraries, like our lives, are labyrinths, what does that make our bookshops or our second-hand bookshops? The ruins of labyrinths? Noel Brookes' shops certainly looked that way.

In the eighties the smaller of the two sites, at 12a Queens Road, had been a goldmine for impoverished students, providing an apparently inexhaustible supply of colourful half-price Pelican Freuds and Arden Shakespeares.[1] Forty thousand titles on four floors and, according to his own advert[2], "Brighton's second most-untidy-bookshop" (which begs an obvious question...and I've yet to find out where he meant). Later, and across the road, the glass-fronted double-unit site could show off a vast collection at its riotous best. In a presentiment of the dismal basement in 2002, piles of books were to be found leaning against straining glass, most of them impossible to recover without crampons, nerves of steel and, of course, permission. Behind that, increasingly precarious shelves, some completely collapsed and only supported by other books, housed science fiction, gay literature and some modern firsts.

This was a dangerous place. Even when you thought you had escaped from the front windows, more sheets of glass reared up in huge cabinets that seemed impossible to open, containing Victorian collections and, if memory serves, a *Shining Pyramid* (a limited Edwardian hardback of Arthur Machen's short story collection). These cabinets would have looked more at home in the Booth Museum, Brighton's Natural History department, where they would have contained queasily realistic Victorian dioramas of taxidermied eagles eating lambs. They were not ideal for displaying books. But then, very little was. Beyond the cabinets lay a maze of bespoke shelving and unopened boxes that constituted the bulk of the stock.

Brookes, like Sandpiper Books in Kensington Gardens today, initially relied on an eye for remainders; books sold by the pallet-load to offset costs by publishers who may have overestimated the market or needed a swift cash injection. The

---

[1] These would then end up sold to The Odd Volume up the road, complete with hung-over notes in the margins.
[2] (driff, 1985) Fascinating, sarcastic, arrogant and occasionally even correct.

joy of discovering almost the complete run of the Quartet Encounters series (translated European fiction and essays) there – not together of course but scattered throughout the shop or, to put it another way, filed correctly – was only slightly offset by the tacit acknowledgement that no-one actually read this stuff enough for it to sell at full price.

Noel Brookes sat on a chair beside what may once have been a desk but was now another book storage area, always with a Sainsbury's shopping bag at his feet. No counter, no till, no computer. No retail trappings at all. He was a tall man with white hair and a florid face, walking a fine line between shabby and smart in ancient bespoke suits.

Right from the start, Brighton was in confusion about Brookes' shop. First an early branch of the Quadrant bookshop was based here, then the less-than-intriguing Barry's Books in 1977. After the next occupant, a theatre bookshop, closed its doors, the space was rented to some kind of nebulous right-wing outfit. Posters and the like were put in the window. Brighton was not happy about this. Bricks were thrown, paint was daubed, and damage was done. Free speech for all but those who oppose free speech. The fascists withdrew. Solstice and Public House suffered at the hands of the local neo-Nazis.

Then the tall taciturn man moved in, labelling his shop front 'N.F. Brookes'. Some people remained rather ignorant and proceeded to spoil a decent little victory by continuing their attacks: an ironic but somehow inevitable reversal of the contemporary attitudes to the Unicorn Bookshop back in 1968. More surplus bricks and the odd bit of damage. Brighton, eh?

There remains a tiny cottage with an exposed outside toilet at the rear of number 12. To this day it looks derelict, abandoned and deeply unpleasant. And it was much the same in Brookes' day when he stored excess stock here in mouldering boxes. Only slightly more accessible was the basement of the main building, which always seemed slightly larger than the rooms upstairs and may have extended out under Queen's Road slightly (or possibly into unfathomable dimensions beyond angled space: you never know). But this was a risky place to visit.

Only a thin strip of wooden floorboards led the brave and inquisitive between dank walls, covered in makeshift shelving and plastered with peeling books, and the monstrous central pile of more books, stacked precariously on ageing cardboard boxes, presumably full of yet more stock. An athletic combination of hands-and-knees and the book dealer's crook-backed, head-sideways shuffle was the only way to risk negotiating this primal maze.

Eventually Brookes had to move across the road and took on the first of the two units that became his main site. It is even possible that he may actually have had permission to knock a large doorway through into the second unit.

Book-runner Pete Scott visited the new shop during the transfer. Noel was stacking cardboard boxes of excess books against the front window, the birth of that memorable and intimidating chaos that amazed and amused so many visitors in later years. "It's only temporary," he called out.

During his time on Queen's Road, reputation and reality found many occasions to contradict one another. Brookes' red face, often taken for the sign of a drinker (and, let's face it, this is not an uncommon side-line in the business), was the result of a skin condition – though he did drink as well. His treatment of customers was legendary but inconsistent. He appeared to be brusque, unhelpful and taciturn: the shop, a disorganised mess. In fact, he knew the exact position of almost every item. He did not suffer fools gladly, but why should anyone? A foreign student once asked him, very politely, if he had any books on the Chinese language.

He said no.

That was all.

There was no attempt to solicit further information or sell something else, no modern notions of intrusive customer service. The student may well have been somewhat surprised that there was to be no further debate on the subject and perhaps sceptical that Brookes could be so definite and inflexible. But Noel was quite certain. Don't waste your time, young man, was the unspoken addendum: I am quite sure. There's nothing here for you.

Some thought his prices too high. Then again, he also gave some of the best prices in town when he bought second-hand books. Many a student had Brookes to thank for a night out, or, but only when absolutely necessary, another text.

He may also have been indirectly but partially responsible for the founding of the magnificent Tartarus Press. Tartarus publishes handsome hardback reprints of weird and supernatural fiction along with *Wormwood*, an excellent literary journal of the fantastic, supernatural and decadent. As a teenager back in the early eighties, Tartarus founder, Ray Russell, used to visit Brighton on a regular basis, scouring second-hand bookshops for traditional teenage fare: existentialism, Sartre, Camus and other miserable French men. He became a favoured customer in the shop, sitting in the uncomfortable chair and being offered lumps of chocolate. One day, possibly as a joke, Brookes gave him a copy of Arthur Machen's *Hill of Dreams* to read. Machen is not really existential, at least not like the French anyway, though this tale of a suicidal Edwardian poet did serve to introduce Ray to the delights of weird fiction. Brookes' gift "...set [me] on a path of publishing and collecting."[1] And he's not looked back since. Now Tartarus publishes everything Machen ever wrote and has, in their turn, introduced a wide audience to many excellent, if faintly obscure, writers.

But where there are facts, there are fancies too. Ray was a good customer but remained blithely ignorant to the fact that Brookes had taken a liking to him. It was only after an offer to come back to Brookes' flat to see some film posters -one of which featured a strapping young lad claiming that he was "not feeling myself tonight" and positioned above the bed apparently- that Ray quickly decided to re-evaluate his own notions of customer service.

---

[1] Ray Russell, private communication.

> Every good bookseller is a multiple personality, containing all the extremes of human feeling. He is an ascetic hermit, he is an erotic immoralist, he is a Papist, he is a quaker, he is a communist, he is an anarchist, he is a savage iconoclast, he is a passionate worshipper of idols."
>
> - *The Pleasures of Literature*
>   John Cowper Powys 1938

And even here the legends continue. I have been told that Noel Brookes had worked for unspecified "government agencies" in his youth. That he had a penchant for rugby players. And that he married a Serbo-Croatian woman, and spoke the language (whichever one that might be), which went some way to explain the preponderance of Eastern European literature in the shop. He certainly spoke excellent Polish, as John Loska's Polish father can attest. John himself remembers Noel's formidable achievements as a cook. He certainly cared for his ageing and sick mother, patiently and for many years.

In the end, and this is as indicative of Brighton culture as any other story, Brookes had to close. The decline began with a 25% off sale which rose to 75% followed by the alleged 'disappearance' of the owner in the spring of 2002 and the abandoning of his remaining books. In the local press, Brookes was reported as having left the shop without warning, the landlord unable to contact him at his last known address. The rumour mill had it that rent was not being paid. Reports in the Argus continued to emphasise the chaos and the enigma while distraught customers letters to the paper paid tribute to the experience of the man and the shop: "Please come back, and add that little dash of colour and sanity to our increasingly colourless world[1]." All this played into the myth of his character very effectively. I know I still saw him striding purposefully around

---

[1] Letter from Richard W. Symonds, *Argus* newspaper, Monday 8th July 2002.

Brighton with Sainsbury's shopping bags on a regular basis. Other dealers remained in contact.

By August 2002, the shop became the site of an art exhibition organised by Caroline Brown which incorporated the remaining stock into low walls of literature like unfilled flower beds or raised graves, depending on your mood. Dealers were asked to take what they liked but leave the white books, as these were part of the display. More books disappeared. Finally the end came. Pete Scott contacted the landlord to ask after the remaining books. Back in the shop for the last time, Pete and Geoff Kinderman, of Brimstones in St. James Street, took away carloads of black sacks filled with books until even they were defeated. Eventually a Spanish furniture company took over the shop unit, selling spectacularly over-priced chunks of MDF and plastic flowers. This lasted barely a year. Since then a branch of a Christian bookshop chain has added joyous compact discs and faceless plaster angels to our incomplete lives. As of January 2010, this too has ceased trading, lost, like Borders, to the grinding erosion of recession.

Brookes died in early 2008. His personal effects were dealt with by the arrival of a long-estranged and previously unseen brother. His own collection of books was purchased by John Loska at Colin Page and Andrew Cummings in Lewes. Towards the end he had begun buying again for some reason. Those books are now dispersed back into the world of collectors.

To be honest, things have never been the same since.

PAST HISTORIC – Holleyman & Treacher

Way back in 1888, Harry and Charles Treacher owned a bookshop, printers and subscription library in the bow-fronted building on the corner of North Street and East Street (1 and 170 North Street and 44 East Street). The area was rebuilt in 1924 to make way for the Hanningtons Department Store, now, in its turn, also only a distant memory.

But Hanningtons was new and exciting when George Holleyman was fourteen years old. He had been in Brighton for ten years, since 1914, and would have seen the demise and destruction of Treacher's emporium. He had always wanted to own a bookshop. Annoyingly, his older brother John beat him to it. While George was still only an assistant at Combridge's in Hove, meeting the likes of Lord Alfred Douglas (who he disliked intensely) and G.K. Chesterton, John ran a bookshop at 70c Preston Street in 1938. Not to be outdone, by 1939 George was at 23 Duke Street (on the corner with West Street), having finally struck out on his own. John and George were brothers and sons of a religious family, regular attendees at the Holland Road Baptist Chapel. In their chosen profession John kept up the spiritual side of things, specialising in books on theology and photography, while George went into the more general antiquarian trade.

Then, with the same superficially bad timing as Kenneth Bredon, came the war: John F. Holleyman & Son went out to 121a Portland Road. George joined up. His first job was as a Military Policeman in the Orkneys where he stayed safe for three years, denuding the tiny islands of any good books. His final military job was as librarian in charge of some seven million images produced by both the RAF and USAAF worldwide. His contribution to the war effort was, despite never leaving Britain, quite significant. He was involved in the successful aerial identification of the V2 bomb launch sites. The war proved advantageous in other ways as well.

> When George Holleyman joined the RAF at the beginning of the war he packed up his entire stock and stored it in lock-up garages. It is said that the increase in its value by the time he was demobilized was the foundation of his success.
> - Anthony Rota[1]

On his return to Brighton, George had more plans, more and better books and help in the form of a member of the bookish Treacher family. He moved a little further down Duke Street to 21a. Treacher owned the building originally but sold it to George for six thousand pounds and then left after a year. Holleyman went on to grow the business into a major antiquarian bookshop. It remained Holleyman & Treacher

---

[1] (Rota, Defending and Regulating the Trade: 100 Years of the Antiquarian Booksellers Association, 2006)

throughout its life. Thanks to that initial investment, the Treacher name has been associated with books in Brighton for over 110 years, albeit obliquely.

George Holleyman had already had a successful career and this continued in parallel with his work as a book dealer. Born in 1910, his family moved to Brighton in 1914 and he never left. His boyish interests in digging and history were ably fostered by Herbert Toms, an assistant of the famous Victorian archaeologist Lieutenant-General Augustus Henry Lane Fox Pitt Rivers and later the curator of Brighton Museums from 1897 until 1937. Despite not acquiring the benefit of a University education, Holleyman still became an important figure in the relatively new discipline of Archaeology, helping to develop techniques in excavation, field survey and aerial archaeology: a variety of expertise ably demonstrated in his classic paper *The Celtic Field System in Southern Britain*, published in the respected archaeological journal *Antiquity* (1935). This remains a significant study of agricultural activity on the South Downs, particularly north of Brighton, during the late Iron Age and Romano-British periods. During the war these aerial survey interpretation skills led him into the RAF. He was a regular at many digs in the area, "digging, washing and cataloguing finds" on a late Bronze Age farm in June 1933 for the Worthing Archaeological Society[1].

As an amateur archaeologist with an excellent reputation, he continued to work on excavations until the sixties. In that time he worked with a keen young digger called Barry Cunliffe. Now Professor Cunliffe and a successful author of many excellent books, he remembers George's odd pirate-style hat worn on all his digs and how they would sit around the camps comparing pot sherds of their own with pictures in the *Sussex Archaeological Collections*: more fun to some than playing cards. Knowing that George was also a book dealer led Barry to intimate that he would like to buy some copies of this respected journal.

---

[1] *Sussex Archaeological Collections* Vol. 75, Brighton History Library.

"When you get home, send me ten shillings and I'll see what I can do," suggested George. This done, Barry received an enormous pile of magazines, for which the postage alone cost far more than his ten shillings. As helpful and generous as he was, George Holleyman still retained something of the old school about him. Apparently he was outraged when the teenage Barry Cunliffe turned up to stay at the tented campsite once. With a girlfriend.

Outside of archaeology, Holleyman seemed to have a knack for profits. After the helpful effects of War on his stock, he made regular trips abroad, especially to South Africa, turning up unusual and valuable finds. He also pulled off a significant literary coup in the early seventies. After the death of Virginia Woolf's husband, Leonard, in 1969 at Monk's House in Rodmell, Sussex, he was called in to value the library. The house had between five and six thousand volumes in it at the time. While some important parts of the collection were sold through Sotheby's the following year, the majority of titles were purchased by and divided between Bow Windows Bookshop in Lewes and George's shop in Brighton. Holleyman & Treacher issued a sale catalogue of 742 items, totalling 1149 volumes, in May 1970 – the *Monk's House Catalogue – Important and Association Books from the Library of Virginia and Leonard Woolf*. Soon after this, Holleyman inspected and purchased yet another Woolf-related collection, the library of Leslie Stephen from 24 Victoria Square, London. The Holleyman & Treacher catalogue for this, issued on March 31st 1972, showed 1875 titles comprising 2681 volumes. That's a lot of books. Almost all of this fine stock has ended up in the Washington State University library in the US, a long way from Bloomsbury and the Sussex Downs.[1]

Holleyman also bought a great deal of stock from the Brighton bookbinder James Sharpe North. North's shop, opened in the late 1890's and originally at 2&3 Prince's Street, had

---

[1] (Holleyman, 1975)

moved to 44 Market Street by the time Holleyman was buying. North, then his son Dudley, ran the shop until the mid-fifties when Holleyman bought all their remaining books, undoubtedly a profitable move from such an established and locally reputable source.

Holleyman & Treacher also had an excellent sheet music department run by John Kite, yet another example of a long-disappeared function of bookshops, new and second-hand. Kite was a partner in the business and kept up a long-running series of music catalogues for an increasing list of discerning customers. He also had an entirely unconnected interest in railway books which added another odd specialisation to the shop's repertoire.

As with most trades, bright young employees can go on to great things, too, if they are lucky, dedicated and good at the job. The shop proved an effective training ground for future booksellers. Raymond Kilgariff was an assistant at Holleyman & Treacher before becoming a partner in the Howes Bookshop in Hastings: a massive and long-lived establishment that has only recently closed. Established by Charles Howes in the 1920s, it was a major stopping place for dealers trawling the South Coast and has provided two Presidents of the Antiquarian Booksellers Association. Ross McKinnon, who went on to start the film bookshop Bioscope in Trafalgar Street, was also a graduate of Holleyman & Treacher.

Mike Astill of Wax Factor remembers attempting to sell two first editions at Holleyman & Treacher. They were, he thought, pretty good examples of the type: a decent T.S. Eliot and a fine Hogarth Virginia Woolf. At the hatch deep within the ill-lit depths of H&T the first response was positive but insubstantial.

"Oh yes," said the quiet, bespectacled gentleman behind the hatch. "They might be, yes, quite possibly we can...the sort of..." and so on. Then a second gentleman appeared, gave them a swift and official once-over, declared them to be "not at all the kind of thing we want," and that was that.

The unrehearsed good-cop/bad-cop routine was played by Michael Kadwell and David Plumtree, the final owners of the shop.

Michael joined George Holleyman in 1964 when John Kite retired. He continued Kite's proven sales of sheet music and, between them, he and George produced dozens of catalogues on their three specialities: Theology, Music, Archaeology and a further General catalogue. It is difficult to imagine the economies and necessity of bookshop catalogues now as almost no-one makes them anymore, relying on the internet instead. Back then, and all the way back to John Metcalf-Morton in the early part of the century, catalogues were something to be treasured and endlessly perused. The experience and range of reference required to make a decent and reliable one was invaluable.

David Plumtree joined Holleyman and Michael in late 1973. George, never averse to a little snobbery, was pleased and somewhat surprised to receive a call from Wing Commander Plumtree, David's father, about the position. David played the bad cop in Mike Astill's little scenario and the story illustrates another classic axiom of second-hand bookselling: most books are rubbish.[1] As much as people like to think they know this (and in today's world of supermarkets, charity shops and paper merchants, it is pretty obvious), when it comes to some battered nineteenth-century hardback with yellowing paper and a bit of leather hanging off it, well, that's rare surely? An antique at the very least.

Not a bit of it. Even if it is rare, which it almost certainly isn't, it is equally likely that no-one actually wants it, making it unsaleable and so next to worthless. Charity shops and amazon sellers take note.

Holleyman & Treacher did not support the traditional labyrinthine confusion of most bookshops. While it still had

---

[1] Although David and Michael could well have been sick of the sight of Virginia Woolf books by that time.

multiple rooms and floors, it was reasonably well-laid out and thoroughly organised - although it did boast some exceptionally high ceilings. Good eyesight and a ladder were required. The memorable sash-window style serving hatch was where a customer brought their hard-won purchases and this opened onto a tiny office. Downstairs in the basement, ladders and stools were once again required for a thorough assessment of the shop's wares.

Book buyers charted their reading development by the succession of rooms visited. Paul O., a regular at the shop for many years, remembers moving from science fiction anthologies on the lower shelves, to English and European literature and then down to the cold basement for foreign languages. Eventually, "the upper stories, with their glass-fronted cabinets and little frequented side rooms...spurred me to begin buying antiquarian books[1]".

George made regular trips to South Africa, bringing back an unusual selection of books, probably buying from rich landowners, finally fed up with Grandfather's ageing Victorian library. As with the Orkneys years before, it was always profitable to plunder somewhere which, while not exactly virgin territory, was certainly off the beaten track for other book dealers.

Time will take its toll though. Whether George decided to sell up and retire when Michael and David expressed an interest in taking over the shop, or vice-versa, is unclear. Holleyman finally retired in 1984. From 1983, he was living in the flat above the shop. David and Michael ran the business. All went well for several years. George retained the established connections with famous people and renowned customers, providing illustrated books for the noted collector Major J.R. Abbey for one. The shop adjusted to the times. While sheet music sales shrank, paperbacks grew, taking over the right wall of the shop by the entrance.

The tail end of the nineties was, however, a bad time for Brighton's books. Read All About It had gone and Public House

---

[1] Personal communication.

closed in 1999. Between those two closures David and Michael called it a day as well in September 1998. The failure of the Net Book Agreement and the changing nature of the market was all coming to a head. Within a few years, Tall Storeys, Brookes, Brimstones in St. James Street and the Trafalgar Bookshop would all be gone.

George Holleyman's extensive collection of books, maps and antiques were sold at auction in Chichester by Henry Adams Auctioneers. Toward the end, amongst the final, general, less inspiring items, John Loska (by then running Colin Page's shop in Duke Street) noticed a small unassuming pamphlet from 1938 of a mere eight pages on the subject of identifying structures from aerial reconnaissance photographs. He didn't buy the lot in question but that may have been the little book that helped George spot the V2 sheds during the war: a work of clear provenance with historical associations and significance. Where is it now?

There is one more thing. David Plumtree has some unfinished business resulting from his time in the shop. Some ashes need delivering. Graham White was an excellent bookseller who worked in Colin Page and was a collector of William Burroughs ephemera. Like Burroughs, White was not averse to a little excessive drug use. Although he stopped all poisonous intake while working at the shop and came out of the other side vastly improved, his body was too damaged to last. Not long ago he died in a pub, choking on a cheese sandwich. With no family to step in, the booksellers rose to the occasion instead. After cremation, he wanted his ashes to be scattered on the grave of the great Edwardian ghost story writer, M.R. James: a final resting place so astutely macabre I wish I'd thought of it myself.

THE HEART OF THINGS
– Ben Hutchinson, Colin Page and John Loska

There is a case to be made for claiming that there remains only one true second-hand bookshop left in Brighton[1]. The green frontage of John Loska's Duke Street shop has been there for nearly thirty-five years. With interesting paperbacks at decent prices on the tables outside, and fine bindings and collectables in the window, the shop still somehow manages to look inherently traditional. Inside there is a spiral iron staircase down to a basement that involves some ducking and opening of

---

[1] With apologies to the Studio Bookshop, Brighton Books, Rainbow and Savery of course.

doors to explore its full potential. The name on the shop board is 'Colin Page'.

But wait a minute. Remember the guy who came round to Bill Butler in 1967 and offered him the shop in Gloucester Road after he had "booted out" his other tenants? That was book-dealer Ben Hutchinson, a man who seemed to own more properties and book depositories in Brighton than you could shake a battered paperback at. A dealer since 1947, he had owned at least four sites since his move to Brighton in 1960: two shops on the book axes of town, Duke Street and Trafalgar Street, the Unicorn site and the last a flat near Preston Street, toward the sea.

A busy man, he published his own magazine on a tiny hand-cranked Roneo duplicator from the flat above his Trafalgar Street shop. Prosaically entitled *Book Collecting & Library Monthly*, it ran to sixty issues between 1968 and 1973. It had a habit of re-introducing largely overlooked nineteenth century authors, such as George Gissing, back into the trade, with the added bonus of increasing the prices of any relevant stock held. A kind of literary fanzine, it also published some of Lee Harwood's poetry.

Long before computers but well after W. J. Smith's Brighton Scrapbooks, Hutchinson had shoe boxes full of bits of paper. This was what passed for his index and filing system. At another extreme, he also collected and eventually sold a personal collection of over 4000 Tauchnitz editions. Tauchnitz - from their founder, Baron Christian Bernhard von Tauchnitz (1816-95) - were a famous Leipzig publisher who had specialised in English language books by British and American authors since 1842. More than a century ahead of their time, these editions were only produced as paperbacks of high quality. This important collection has ended up, like so many others, at the University of Texas. In his old suits and with a perpetually half-smoked roll-up hanging from his mouth, Ben Hutchinson's traditional philosophy was "buy cheap and sell dear". Richard Cupidi dubbed him "the last Dickensian bookseller in Brighton".

By 1979, under constant threat from a long-suffering spouse ("it's me or the books!"), Hutchinson decided to emigrate to Australia. He asked a book-dealer friend of his, Ken Smith, recently uprooted from Harrow, to clear the 30,000 books accumulated in the various flats. Smith agreed on condition "that I could stay on in the flat above Ben's shop in Brighton...I spent a very pleasant few months sorting out the books."[1] The shop at 42 Trafalgar Street, where the magazine was printed, had only opened on Saturdays anyway, while the Duke Street site...well, this is where Colin Page comes in.

Colin and his brother, Brian, trained as motor mechanics under their father in his Port Hall Road garage after the war. Eventually, both brothers decided this was not for them. Colin had gone into George Sexton's shops and seen the old man in his hat and coat, huddled round a one-bar electric fire, shouting at customers. Sexton was still selling decent antiquarian books at very reasonable prices at that time, so Colin got into the habit of buying some up and then selling them around to the other booksellers. There were bargains to be found in those days. This all seemed to go reasonably well and there could certainly be a living in it, with perseverance. Stepping up, Colin went to Sotheby's to learn the trade. There were two distinct auction rooms back then: the posh books still went through the New Bond Street rooms where the company's reputation had been established, while everything else went through Hodgson's Rooms in Chancery Lane, part of the Sotheby's empire since 1968. Colin went into buying fine books that were slightly imperfect from the latter. Perhaps they had a title page missing or were otherwise only slightly damaged. It made little difference to the book overall but this is where perfectionism steps in to play games with economics. Imperfections put these otherwise fine books beyond the pale for serious collectors, thus their prices at auction were considerably lower than might be expected and could be snapped up for a song. There were other tricks too.

---

[1] Kenneth Smith, interviewed for *The Bookdealer* by Sheila Markham in 1999.

The cheaper lots tended to be sold after 'lunch' which largely consisted of a great deal of beer. So the afternoons were sleepy times. A man with his wits about him (and a carefully developed acquaintance with either the main auctioneer, Lord John Kerr, then head of Sotheby's Book department, or W.B."Mr Wilfrid" Hodgson, a direct descendant of one of the founders) could easily pick up a succession of quality lots without even waking his competitors from their slumbers.

The books could then be sold to bookshops and dealers, at a small profit but with the benefit of constant education in the trade, especially from helpful locals like George Holleyman. Eventually Colin and Brian opened a small shop in Station Road, Lewes, naming it 'Kokoro' from Brian's particular interest in all things Japanese. The name means 'heart and soul' or 'feeling', 'the heart of things'. Colin's books aside, it was certainly unusual to find a Japanese specialist in Lewes, that bastion of traditional English values. On the other hand, the inhabitants of Lewes do have a tendency to burn effigies of random enemies and roll flaming barrels down their main street every November 5th. So perhaps many things are possible in the heart of Britain.

After one more move within Lewes, above Reeves the photographers on the High St, reputedly the oldest professional photographers in Britain, Kokoro moved to Brighton in 1976. And, thanks to Ben Hutchinson, into 36 Duke Street.

"Don't change anything," was all Hutchinson said when the brothers moved in. The shop, a former bakery, had been slowly and inconsistently fitted with esoteric shelving, erected as and when required and as cheaply as possible. Upright planks were attached to the walls at right angles, then six inch nails hammered through them to support shelves as best they could. When the weight of stock got too much for this dismayingly bespoke system, which it unfailingly did, the nails would bend downwards to violently caress the hands of any unsuspecting investigator. In the toilet there was no toilet paper, simply a selection of books with no covers and a dawning realisation.

How those particular books were chosen remains a mystery, as did the state of the plumbing.

"Don't change anything."

Colin and Brian gutted the place. They replaced all the lethal shelves and fitted the spiral staircase, turning the basement into a decent space and beginning over twenty years of trading. Presumably they also indulged in toilet paper. Colin got to put his name on the Duke Street shop, where it remains.

George Holleyman, only a short browse away on the other side of street, was perfectly happy with the competition and thought the situation was good for the book trade in general: "But I never want to see you in my shop again." There would be no more deals between them, no buying and selling that close to home. It was a professional solution to any future problems.

Over time Brian's specialisation separated and moved into the new East Street Arcade in the South Lanes. As in Lewes, this small shop stood out, too. Among the fashionable boutiques, shiny new floors and artificial lighting, there were fossil dinosaur eggs in this window, sitting solid and immutable among Japanese prints.

Colin was still looking ahead. He bought a computer in 1979 when they were still the size of a washing machine and about as reliable. It was a Commodore Pet, had a 16K memory and came with floppy discs galore. He wanted to create a full catalogue and "tailor-made lists to match customer's interests"[1] and needed someone to type in the entries.

John Loska couldn't type and told Colin so at his interview. He had finished a degree in Mathematics at Sussex University and had been buying and selling books in Brighton for a few years already. His tastes, Sir Walter Scott and Lord Lytton (of "It was a dark and stormy night..." infamy) may have been a little dry but books of this sort could still be bought for surprisingly little money. As with Colin's imperfect lots, it

---

[1] John Loska - *The Mechanics of Bookselling*, interviewed by Sheila Markham in *Rare Books*.

provided a decent introduction to the business. Luckily for Brighton, Colin did offer John the job. He hoped it would take six weeks.

The machine crashed constantly.

Everything took much longer than anticipated.

John and Colin, however, got on very well. First he was offered a permanent position. In the late eighties, he became a partner. Then, when Colin retired in 1999, John took over the business. Ironically, John's books are not to be found on the internet, making Colin Page one of the few shops too have resisted the descent into virtuality. He is right in thinking that this makes the shop more interesting for customers. Once again, the physical presence of a book-buyer (and book seller) can make browsing worthwhile. On the other hand, he might just be fed up with computers.

John and his small team work hard. Keeping on top of an unpredictable and unstable market involves a good deal of travelling to auctions and private sales accompanied by the regular exercise of an inexhaustible reservoir of expert knowledge, supplemented by Colin Page dropping in for tea once a week. From the consistently distracting paperbacks outside the shop, through the fine bindings, down the spiral stairs and all the way to the antiquarian rarities that never have time to settle on bookshop shelves, Colin Page remains one of the finest second-hand and antiquarian bookshops in Britain.

Brighton is lucky to have it: as can be seen from the next chapter...

BRIGHTON: A SURVEY

> There have always been a number of bookshops, and a strong nucleus holds its own against the general erosion nationally. Costs here are just as high, but the general attraction of the town as a place to live and the stimulation of healthy competition has infused fresh blood, so that new shops replace those which fall by the wayside.
>
> — Roy Harley Lewis on Brighton
> *The Book Browser's Guide*, David & Charles
> 1975

That is the sad side of book-hunting; far more shops disappear than new shops open. Even Brighton is not what it was.

- Graham Greene, from his introduction to David Low's *With All Faults* 1973

1969 - A *Directory of Dealers in Second-hand and Antiquarian Books in the British Isles 1969-1971* - Sheppard Press, 1969.
  - 11 entries - 0 left
  - Three of these are specialists in printing history, cars and travel or maritime books.

1975 - *The Book Browsers Guide: Britain's Second-hand and Antiquarian Bookshops* - Roy Harley Lewis, David & Charles.
  - 7 entries - 0 left
  - All seven entries are definitively and unquestionably 'pure', though general, second-hand and/or antiquarian bookshops.[1]

1985-86 - *Driffs Guide to All the Second-hand and Antiquarian Bookshops in Britain* - Driffield, BCM Driffield, London.
  - 12 entries - 2 left
  - One of the two extant shops is Kemp Town Books, which is not second-hand or antiquarian.

1996 - *Skoob Directory of Second-hand Bookshops in the British Isles* (6th edition) - general editor M. P. Ong, Skoob Books Ltd.
  - 14 entries - 3 left
  - Of the original fourteen, one is Kemp Town Books again, while another is Wax Factor which also sells as much music as it does books.

---

[1] As are the two mentioned in Lewes, both of which still survive today (the Fifteenth Century Bookshop and Bow Windows).

- Of the three remaining, one is Kemp Town Books and one is Wax Factor.

2009 - Online bookshop guide for the University of Sussex – John Shire 2009
- 22 entries. However...
- 2 are market stalls, 3 are in the covered market (Snooper's Paradise), 5 are new or remainder shops[1], 3 are books plus others things (music, magazines, games, comics, figures etc), 4 are charity bookshops, leaving...
- 5 purely second-hand and/or antiquarian shops[2]

There is nothing left from 1975.

The number of general second-hand bookshops rose to a maximum in the mid-nineties.

Currently only five still exist.

There are debatable issues here, of course. The owners of Studio Books and Brighton Books, two of the five survivors, have been in the business for years, just not in Brighton. Colin Page opened in 1976. In the vast covered market of Snooper's Paradise, there is the consistently interesting Invisible Books stand and at least two other book-only stalls. Driffield, despite a well-deserved reputation for splenetic thoroughness, could not find all the bookshops in Brighton at the time of his tours (Avalon Books, for example, though that might have been a blessing for them). The Skoob Directory authors certainly didn't, while in 2010 I have the advantage of almost daily checks on the state of the business, so my inclusion of market stalls, remainder outlets and charity shops could be seen as cheating. Or significant.

There is one bookshop that is not mentioned in any of the above listings. James and Sheila Keeble have run Two-Way Books at 54 Gardner Street since 1964. In the main, their shop has a relatively small stock and deals only in paperbacks and

---

[1] As of 2011 Borders, the Works and Bookzone have now disappeared too.
[2] Colin Page, Savery Books, Brighton Books, Rainbow Books and Studio Books. And Savery do antiques too.

magazines but it is an extraordinary survivor. A small warning though: their price stickers do not come off without a fight. David Paine started work here but later moved on to open up all manner of other stores in the same street, some of which still survive. It was deliberate and focused competition, distinctly painful for a while. At one point David opened an entire shop that sold thousands of units of remainder stock for 10p. The Graphic Novel shop, originally an offshoot of Dave's Comics, has grown into one of the finest in the country, featuring, to its eternal credit, a bewildering selection of independent products.

There are many ways of telling stories about Brighton's bookshop history: it's easy to forget some important ones. Sydney Street has seen more than its fair share of books come and go.

And let's get some wider perspective here too.

Before 1975 the difference between second-hand and new outlets was important and pronounced, more so than in the past, when Combridge's and Bredon's had second-hand departments of their own and second-hand bookshops were mainly antiquarian bookshops only. Even Unicorn had an unusually extreme range in the sixties, from the 1684 volume "...in old calf, very shabby and with no lettering on the spine..." purchased by David Low[1] to the newest poetry pamphlet straight off the local press or the latest Grove Press release from America. Unicorn is not mentioned as a second-hand dealer in a 1969 Sheppard guide to bookshops. The Net Book Agreement was in full force and publishers had yet to increase print runs beyond economic sanity. The price difference and quality difference between hardbacks and paperbacks was significant and why a book got published in one format or the other counted for something as well. For the general public, at least, antiquarian books, and possibly books in general, were not that popular or in any way sought after. Richard and Judy day-dreamed wistfully about jobs in television.

Driffield picked viciously at and on the insular, unhelpful and disingenuous second-hand book market of the

---

[1] (Low, 1973)

eighties. Iain Sinclair characterised and caricatured him, the dealers, runners and bookshop owners in *White Chappell Scarlet Tracings*, exposing "...the tremulous and corrupt, but essentially trivial, sub-continent of bookselling."[1]

In 1991 Dillons and Waterstone's began to discount books. By the time of the demise of the Net Book Agreement in 1997, new books effectively flooded the market; print runs increased, popular titles were sought after and actively promoted by all manner of media, and all this was available in big new stores and even supermarkets.

> Before I could read, almost a baby, I imagined that God, this strange thing or person I heard about, was a book. Sometimes it was a large book standing upright and half open and I could see the print inside but it made no sense to me. Other times the book was smaller and inside were sharp flashing things.
>
> - Jean Rhys, *Smile Please*, 1979.

Also, from roughly the same time, the Internet made its presence felt. First simply a new medium, by now the virtual arena has made drastic and permanent changes to the economics, distribution and quality of books and bookshops. The new book trade argues over the price and accessibility of e-books and the quality of e-book readers, pursuing the hope of Ipod-style success with eyes for ears. A single vowel change is all that is required. Print-on-demand (POD) options confuse quality and availability while an effective and efficient POD machine haunts the nightmares of publishers and bookshop staff but gleams in the dreams of executives: though even now the chatter about POD already seems to have been circumvented by digital delivery via Kindles, Ipads and Androids. Second-hand dealers disappear into the anonymity of the World Wide Web, where

---

[1] (Sinclair, 1987)

previously rare titles appear with shocking regularity and long-term professionals vie with stay-at-home mums listing their cookery books[1] on Amazon for unlikely prices. Now anyone can deal in books on the internet, breaking down Driffield's "corrupt" markets with a whole different style of corruption.

The market will shake it all down, separating the sheep from the chaff, if that's how you believe the market works. The Internet marketplace (mainly Amazon but also Ebay and Abe) only seems to head one way. In general, books are getting cheaper as a result of immense competition in the face of shrinking demand.

Small publishers debate the nature of the new economic and distribution systems. Some are POD only while others refuse to go down that road. The POD poetry publishers, Salt, are struggling, as is Dedalus, specialists and award winners in translated European fiction. Both have had their Arts Council funding cut so drastically that they may not survive. We do, however, have the Olympics to look forward to. Not that the two things are connected in any way, of course.

Borders and Books etc have both passed on recently leaving only one major chain bookseller to the high streets of the nation. But Waterstone's too have made staff redundant and are closing stores while attempting to centralise distribution through their 'Hub' warehouse, run by another company entirely. Both these things happened at Virgin Retail Ltd, which was very effective at hiding its huge debts. Virgin then became zavvi after a management buy-out, which then went into administration, and which finally died, making me and several hundred other people redundant. All of which gave me the time to write this.

Silver linings and all that.

> Also [the book trade] is a humane trade which is not capable of being vulgarized beyond a certain point. The combines can never squeeze

---

[1] Or, for that matter, any piece of printed matter that comes to hand in these credit-crunched times.

the small independent bookseller out of existence as they have squeezed the grocer and the milkman.[1]

It's not often you get the chance to accuse George Orwell of misplaced optimism.

In Brighton, then, the last man standing is the multi-storied branch of HMV-owned Waterstone's, now attempting to turn around recent failings by reverting to an older business model of more independence for stores but struggling to rediscover the experience and knowledge that once made it successful. Remaining at the edges of town are City Books and Kemp Town Books with their loyal clientele and pet authors, both local and national.

The second-hand city dwindles but does not disappear. Colin Page, that fine figure of a bookshop, innocently challenges the flighty restaurants and boutiques of Duke Street with its very constancy. Brighton Books and Sandpiper provide high quality merchandise on Kensington Gardens. Rainbow Books is a reminder of the heyday of Trafalgar Street. David's, Wax Factor and Two-Way Books maintain variety with collectables, games, magazines and music in the mix. Studio Books is a haven of tranquillity, far from the madding crowd, as is Savery Books, though shrunken from its former entire-house-of-books glory.

I find that I write these things in a 'where did it all go wrong?' tone but that is perhaps only a superficial way to understand these manifold changes. On the positive side, the internet has allowed dealers to re-market their stock to a far wider audience at little cost. The large and unpredictable overheads of rent and 'public' storage can be replaced by the more manageable ones of IT upkeep and postage. Some places do both. Others, like Brimstones, have disappeared from St.

---

[1] (Orwell, 1936)

James's Street (where it was from 1990 to 2000), into the countryside, to exist only on the net.[1]

Small publishers now have access to the biggest and perhaps most effective marketing tool in history to promote their product. But this does put them on an apparently level playing field with everyone else, competing for attention and money. But where money is concerned, the field isn't really level at all. Exclusive deals with supermarkets and heavy discounting account for the majority of business done these days. Small, independent publishers, unable to join in these economies of scale, are left with the infinite space of the web, where they must stand out like a needle in a haystack (of needles), and the shrinking number of shops that are becoming increasingly dislodged from the country's high streets. Customers expect books to be spectacularly cheap these days without quite understanding the economics or the consequences. Many wondered at the 'half-price offer' that began the excellent sales of Tony Blair's memoirs from its first release date, wondering if the 'low' price was a result of poor sales or at least poor sales projections.

On the contrary. That is old-school thinking. Like Jamie Oliver's cookery book from Christmas 2009, these new titles have a very high Recommended Retail Price (another outmoded indicator of value) but almost none of them are expected to be sold at that price. All will be included in massive bulk discounts passed onto the consumer from day of release. Fine for the customer but doesn't it all seem a little underhand? A product of bad faith economics based on out-dated systems and business plans? Does it remind anyone of the music business? Perhaps it is only those directly involved or personally concerned who consider this subsequent devaluing of the nature of the book itself relevant to society at large.

The relationship between the importance of books to the public, on the one hand, and the importance of the written word in society, on the other, is the measure of the value of bookshops. In a relatively short history as consumable objects,

---

[1] www.brimstones.co.uk

books have moved from being rare, expensive and significant through a long line of changes in accessibility, function, aims and production until, perhaps finally, a college in the US is pronouncing itself not "bookless" but "paperless", as it disposes of books in a library and shifts entirely to a virtual, e-book, interface source.

But I like to deal, as do many others, with books as discrete, physical objects that can continue to exist outside of a power failure, as another carbon-based form that can survive the electro-magnetic pulse of a nuclear explosion, if not the explosion itself. Books as objects, not just content. Books as decoration, insulation, obstruction, not the result of sorting a data cloud.

> When he finished a book, he would throw it in the fireplace. "Why do you do that?"...Well, he'd finished with them, why else? A book burning slowly in the grate, charring slowly, only gradually breaking into flame. He would sit by the fire sipping his scotch in the alluring light of the burning book.
>
> - Dashiell Hammett in Diane Johnson's
>   *The Life of Dashiell Hammett*,
>   Chatto & Windus 1984

To continue with questions, is Brighton a particularly good indicator of this history? Does it make a good case-study?

Like any new city, Brighton never had a deep background in the book trade. There were no famed printers or legendary streets from the seventeenth century here that have passed into publishing legend. As ever, it is too close to London for that. It was really only later that the then-town became a place of alternatives: when books became one of the more important weapons in the war of ideas, as Cowper Powys imagined. What Brighton does have is an active, mobile (to the point of transient), artistic and above all literate population that supports bookshops as best they can. With the help of the odd visionary American trained on London streets and a radical new University, all that potential flourished. A special place certainly, as so many discover, but not exceptional in the world of books.

Now, with a reputation firmly based on openness, variety, lifestyles and hedonism -all of which would have been thoroughly appreciated by previous inhabitants- do books still have a significant place in this city by the sea? Is the new tide coming in too quickly? Blogging professionals and early-users of cutting edge technology write with increasing frequency (and probably from trains, balloons or up mountains) of the take-up and increasing advantages of wholesale digital delivery. Is the book doomed? Can bookshops, new then second-hand, do anything but meekly follow?

APOCRYPHA

> They talk it, but they will never write it. The major part gets forgotten and lost forever...the best stories are those you don't dare relate.
>
> - Oswald Frederick Snelling
>   *Rare Books and Rarer People:*
>   *some personal reminiscences of 'the trade'*
>   Werner Shaw, 1982

Reading Brighton like a book is not an easy proposition. The plots are inconclusive and faintly preposterous while the wide cast of unlikely characters make the tales difficult to follow. Sometimes it requires a certain 'suspension of disbelief', as the critics say.

Inevitably, too, there are numerous rumours, tales and nebulous facts that I have failed to drag into the light of day. These failures and fantasies alone go to show how much can still be done in a little town -or, if you insist, a big city- if you look hard enough and under the right rocks. I never quite got to the bottom of the vast alternative master bookshop slap bang in the centre of town at 24 North Road, proposed by Richard Cupidi with help from either Paul Bonnet or Tony Miller. To be honest, perhaps I just wanted there to be more to it.

I haven't found the place to mention anything about the Courthouse Steps bookshop where I have seen the proprietor boiling a kettle on top of steaming piles of books, oblivious to damage. The Courthouse Steps building is reputed to have a secret passage in its backyard that leads to the kitchens of the Royal Pavilion, something else I'd like to explore, even if it is full of rats now.

It would have been cheap and fundamentally incorrect to continue with my previous title for the Holleyman & Treacher chapter, taken from Driffield -"Just Fucking Die You Boring Bastards"- after enjoying the company of David Plumtree and Michael Kadwell. I only mention it now because I'm always a little disappointed by books without a modicum of swearing. Besides, this assessment is apparently based on Driffield[1] parking his bike outside and looking in through the window only.

Restricting myself to one young city has brought into sharp relief the significance and history of other local areas, particularly nearby Lewes, which seems much more adept at cultivating and supporting second-hand bookshops than cosmopolitan Brighton. I am also sad to say that I never visited the enormous Howes Bookshop in Hastings before it closed down.

I could not find out whether George Sexton or James Thorpe owned the two storey book warehouse in the tiny dead end of Ship Street Court. So far I have successfully managed to avoid any mention of neoist novelist Stewart Home and the publisher R.A. Caton, both of whom have Brighton stories to be told. There is also the surprisingly tuneless man who discovered Kate Bush back in 1973 but I can't go into that either.

From America, Paul Garner has told me of Ruth and Richard Moseley who used to run a bookshop in Brighton during the late seventies. They also published limited prints runs of poetry, including *Brother Wolf*, an early collection by Barry MacSweeney for Turret Books. Bill Butler and Adrian Henri also had collections published by Turret, all in 1972.

As to publishers and presses in general, there is another book to be written. From George Higgens' hand-built press at Hove in the 1920s (Oak, Ash & Thorn Press) through Combridge's own publications up to the original Snake River Press[2], there are vast bibliographic minefields to explore. Professor John Spiers founded the award-winning Harvester Press from offices in Ship Street in 1970. He wrote the essay on George Gissing that Ben Hutchinson published in his little magazine and went on to publish his own, rather larger, *The Rediscovery of George Gissing* (1971). Luckily local presses and

---

[1] My various presentations of Driffield's name only vary as much as his own, by the way.
[2] The name and logo are now used by Peter Bridgewater, a student of the original founders, for his range of local Sussex books.

independent works can find outlets in a range of Brighton shops. The new Snake River Press and Queenspark books are in the Brighton History Centre while Dave's Comics/The Graphic Novel Shop and the Permanent Bookshop showcase an eclectic mix of artistic obscurities. Other local specialists include the children's bookshop, the Book Nook, in Hove (a hive of activity), and the English Language Bookshop, for foreign students and their teachers, in George Street, Kemp Town.

Speaking of art, I've not found space for the tale of the fake Churchill signatures either.

There is a nameless second-hand bookshop near Preston Park that I have been saving as a secret from myself. I'll go there one day when all this is over.

The notorious book dealer, Charles Traylen, kept a shop-cum-store in Brighton for a time after the Second World War and he dealt with both Georges Holleyman and Sexton. He made his name through some rather contentious transactions with London auction houses and with his shop in Guildford. There is a story of some faked Thomas Hardy pamphlets, a mere five in all and very rare, connected to both the Howes Bookshop and Holleyman: but such things melt into air with excessive scrutiny.

Who set fire to the Josef K bookshop in Surrey Street in 2002 and why? It is fairly likely that a good many of my science fiction paperbacks went up in smoke, having sold them off there not long before. Somehow I doubt that had anything to do with it, though.

Hundreds, possibly thousands, of people have their own unique memories of Unicorn and Public House. I am certain that I have barely scratched the muralled surfaces of those shops. Both deserve full biographies of their own.

Other things that remain occluded are the hands of change in Adam Ball's shop, the extent of Edwin Morley's interest in the occult and what happened to Vortex. The local Freemasons, despite having an easily accessible website with an enquiry section and, no doubt, worryingly comprehensive archives, did not deign to reply to any requests whatsoever about the Metcalfe-Mortons and their Masonic predilections. Although I suppose I shouldn't be too surprised about that.

Who ran Collie Books or Elmo Books or oversaw the demise of Tall Storeys? There was a bookshop on the West Pier at some point. If anyone can sort out the many properties of Quinton Edwards - libraries, bookshops or whatever they were - they are a better man than I.

There is surprisingly little mention of actual books in the previous pages. However, I did find something that successfully encapsulates both local names and sites, all already mentioned, with, perhaps, a subtle presentiment, indicative of that Brighton culture and atmosphere that remains at once pervasive and elusive. In the Rare Books & Special Collections of the Jubilee Library, there is an anonymous, slim, blue volume called, accurately if not imaginatively, *Poems*. It was published in Brighton by H. & C. Treacher in 1868 and was later presented to the Brighton Public Library by James Thorpe Esq. (owner of the Ship Street bookshop before George Sexton) in April 1904. The poems, dutifully dedicated to the anonymous author's wife (identified only by her initials - E.J.W.L.), have corrections added in the author's own hand: a word changed here, a sense adjusted there.

Despite this, they are still rubbish - even the initially intriguing 'Perverts', which simply appears to be about getting confused by ancient foreigners or something. I have no idea. Who reads nameless Victorian poets any more anyway? So moving on to more important concerns...

While worrying about accuracy and rigour in previous chapters is entirely legitimate, it is this current section that is becoming the most difficult to manage and for two very different reasons. The first is obvious. This is a never-ending story: the more I see, the more I see there is to see, as the old adage goes. On the other hand, and this comes as a surprise given the traditional inertia of the book trade, I'm finding it hard to keep up. Since I began this study, Borders UK, Waterstone's only real high street rival, has disappeared. Howes Bookshop in Hastings closed after almost 80 years of trading. Currently (early 2011)

British Bookshops/Sussex Stationers has entered administration after a disastrous Christmas showing, while Waterstone's are making Head Office staff redundant and closing at least 20 stores this year. W.H. Smith's, that ancient stalking-horse of the book trade, has bought several of the British Bookshops sites already.

The biggest loss, and the one which prompted this book in the first place, was the death of Noel Brookes in early 2008. I overheard Hamilton Wilson of Sandpiper informing another customer about this sad event in January and interrupted the conversation with an entirely inappropriate: "Damn, suppose I'd better get on with it then." I don't even have a decent photograph of the labyrinthine interiors of either of his shops.

And I promised not to say who stabbed someone in the neck with a biro.

To all those who now think I've been fanciful when I should have been factual, and vice versa, I have three words: revised second edition[1]. Set the record straight and put me in my place.

...I was not really the bookseller, but an eccentric gentleman masquerading as such...

Over Bemerton's - E.V. Lucas 1908.

---

[1] An e-book, of course.

BIBLIOPOLYGRAPHY
– A Neologism of Brighton Bookshops

> ...[H]ad we, indeed, possessed all possible leisure for research, every available material, and a space thoroughly unlimited, it is most probable that the result would have been distinguished chiefly for its bulk, tediousness and monotony.
>
> - *A History of Booksellers:*
> *The Old and the New*
> Henry Curwen 1873.

An innately ridiculous, unhelpful and incomplete list, this only goes to show the extent of what the book trade used to be, from roughly the latter quarter of the nineteenth century until now, in one small town on the South Coast of England. If it serves to jog anyone's memory or someone comes across a long-lost ancestor, so much the better.

Closed – second-hand
Adam Ball Antiquarian Books Ltd - 31 Trafalgar Street – 1985-mid 90s.
Avalon Books Ltd - 88 Gloucester Road, then Jubilee Shopping Hall – 1986-1989.
Book Mark - 91 Dyke Road – est. 1994.
Bookmark – 7 Powis Square – est. 1974, private premises.
Booklands - 56 Gardner Street.
Brighton Workers Bookshop -37 Gloucester Road. Early 70's.
Brighton Bargain Books -33 St James' Street.
Brimstones - 33 St. James Street. 1990 – 2000 then moved to unit 6, Sewell Farm, Lewes, www.brimstones.co.uk
N.F. Brookes - 12a Queens Road, 124 Queens Road – 1981-2002.
Mary Brown - Books and clothes and knick-knacks, near Brighton Station, now the Eco Centre/Funeral Directors.

Brunswick Exchange - 41 Brunswick St. East, Hove.
Leslie Thomas Buckingham – 40 St. James Street – c.1936.
Collie Books - 34 Kensington Gardens – c.1996.
Courthouse Bookshop -181 Edward Street – c.1994-1997.
David's Book Exchange -3 Sydney Street – comics and collectables still extant.
J. Elder – 20 Bristol Road, est 1876.
J. Ellison – 50 Meeting House Lane – c.1936.
Elmo Books - 31 Sydney Street – c.2005.
W.F. Fowler – 18 Marlborough Place, est. 1918.
George Sexton Books Ltd - 110 North Street, 14 Dyke Road and 53 Ship Street – est.1913-1976.
Holleyman & Treacher (& Son) - 21a Duke Street – est.1937-1998. Also *Holleyman & Son* - 121b Portland Road, Hove – c.1950.
Ben Hutchinson - 42 Trafalgar Street – est. 1961.
A.M. Jackman – 10 Air Street, est. 1925.
Josef K/Sancho Panza -Surrey Street, now stall at Saturday market.
Kenny Lane - 52 Blatchington Road, Hove – est.1960.
Marlborough Bookshop - 17 Marlborough Place – c.1918. *Out of Print* in 1978, also 103 St. George's Road and *Peterson & Short* by 1980.
George William Marsh – 21 Upper Gardner Street – c.1950.
A. Metcalfe-Morton (The Old Bookhouse) – 44 Gloucester Street, est 1922.
E. North – 30 Church Road, Hove – 1896.
The Odd Volume - 53 Upper Gloucester Road – 1979-1987.
Oxfam Bookshop - 58 Church Road.
Picture Books - 91 Dyke Road and 88 St. James Street – est.1976.
Quadrant – 12a Queens Road.
Quintos of Brighton - 34 Duke Street – c.1986.
Renaissance Books – 52a North Road – est.1979.
Rowan-Robinson - 36 Montpelier Road.
Sandilands aka *Passe Partout*– The Lanes – 19th century.
Sheppard's Bookshop – 22 Trafalgar Street – est.1956.
Shrimpton & Cookis – Market Place Post Office – c.1936.

W. J. Smith - 41,42,43 North Street – 1860s-1911.
Smith's (C.S. Dickson) – 20 King's Road – est.1895-1950s?.
C.F. Smith – 50 The Lanes.
Stanhope & Co. – 20 Bristol Road, est. 1876.
Studio 4 - 4 Little Western Street.
Symposium Bookshop - 12 Market Street – c.1973-1977
Tall Storeys - 88 St. James Street – c.1979-2000 under several owners.
Templar Books - 8 Coldean Lane.
Tempus Fugit, later *Bennetts* - 71a Western Road, Hove –c.1969.
Tenpenny Book Exchange - 95 North Road – c.1987.
James Thorpe – 53 Ship Street, est. 1868.
S.W. Tidy – 13 Ship Street Gardens, est. 1912.
Trafalgar Bookshop - 44 Trafalgar Street – est.1979.
E. van Dam – 3 Bevendean Crescent – c.1936 – specialised in manuscripts!
Mrs Elizabeth Vigor – 14 Oxford Street – c.1950.
Ye Olde Booke Shoppe - 1 Duke Street – c.1911.

Extant – second-hand
Brighton Books - 18 Kensington Gardens.
Colin Page – 36 Duke Street – est.1976.
Rainbow Books - 28 Trafalgar Street – est.1998.
Savery Books – 257 Ditchling Road – est.1993.
Studio Bookshop - 68 St. James Street. Previously *Collected Works* in Dulwich c.1985, *The Bloomsbury Bookshop* and the *Bec Bookshop* in Tooting Bec before Brighton.
Two Way Books - 54 Gardner Street – est.1964.
Wax Factor - 24 Trafalgar Street – est.1982.

Closed – new
Autobooks Ltd – 76 Bennett Road – est.1948.
John Baird – 195 Church Road, Hove (prop. S.R. Ellis), est. 1900.
Barry's Bookshop - 12a Queen's Road – 1970s?

Bernadette's - 29 Bristol Road - c.1977.
Bioscope - 27 Trafalgar Street est.1972 - film specialist.
Blue Arrow Book Co. - 44 Gloucester Street - pre-1927.
Booksmith - 55 Churchill Square - c.1977.
The Book Parlour - 54 Church Street - est.1968.
Boot's Booklover's Library - 158-162 Western Road - pre-1927.
K. J. Bredon's - 10/10a East St, at 70 East St for second-hand and 22 Prince Albert St in 1968 - est.1937.
Brighton Books - 12 Market Street - early 1970s.
C. J. Buckland - 112 St. James Street - c.1927.
Collector's Bookshop - 32 Gloucester Road - c.1980.
Combridges - 56 Church Road, Hove - est.1901.
G Book Centre - 50 Queen's Road - c.1977.
Fisher Nautical - 130 Hollingbury Park Avenue - est.1966. Postal business only.
Forty Sutherland - 8 Egremont Place - c.1978.
J. Hamilton - 24 Queen's Road - c.1930.
Hatchard's in Hannington's Department Store, North Street.
E. Homewood & Co. - 45 Dyke Road - c.1930. Their Library mosaic can still be seen here.
International Bookshop - 14 Imperial Arcade (and 52 Charing Cross Road) - c.1936.
O.H. Leeney - 7 Cranbourne Street, est. 1920.
J. Murdoch - 109 St. James Street - c.1980.
James Sharpe North - bookbinder, 2 & 3 Prince's Place then 44 Market Street - 1890-1950s.
North Laine Books - 72 Trafalgar Street - c.1980.
Out! - 4-7 Dorset Street - c.2000.
Plus-One Books - 151 Lewes Road - c.1981.
Portland Centre - 16 Preston Street - c.1980.
Practical Books - 14a Western Road, Hove - est.1962-2003.
Public House Bookshop - 21 Little Preston Street - 1973-1999.
Quadrant - 16 Imperial Arcade - early 1970s.
Read All About It - East Street - 1979-1997.
Robinson's Bookshop - 50-52 Meeting House Lane and at Brighton College of Education in 1976 at Falmer.

Solstice - 28 Trafalgar Street – 1977-1982.
Susan Reynolds Books - 72 Western Road – c.1980.
Theatre Bookshop - 26 New Road – est.1962.
John Tiranti Ltd. – PO Box 151, est. 1895. Agents abroad: Tice & Lynch, New York.
Transpersonal Bookshop - 19 Stirling Place, Hove – c.1978.
Unicorn Bookshop - 50 Gloucester Road – 1967-1975.
Vortex – near Preston Circus – late 1970s?
J. Walser – 37 & 78 Western Road – c.1927.
Wilbury Bookshop - 69a Church Road, Hove – mid-1980s?
Windhorse Emporium - 18 George Street – c.1980.

Extant – new
City Books – Western Road – est.1986.
Dave's Comics/The Graphic Novel Shop – 5 Sydney Street.
Kemptown Books - 91 St. Georges Street – est.1973.
The Permanent Bookshop at The Permanent Gallery – 20 Bedford Place.
Sandpiper Books – Kensington Gardens.

Dealers
Charles W. Traylen - 18 Ship Street in 1949.
Mrs G. Folkes - 40 Islingword Road – c.1968.
Frederick William Fowler - 18 Marlborough Place in 1949.
G. & C. Gidley - 79 London Road and 92 George Street, Hove, in 1954. Also G.R. Gidley at 47 London Road in 1930.
R.T. Gray – 11 Church Street and 9 Gloucester Street – c.1936.
Hyland Charles Harnett – 3 Lorne Road – c.1936.
Harold Heritage - 56 Queen's Road – c.1936.
E. Martin - 2a Sussex Heights, St. Margaret Place in 1980.
Miss Dorothy Penhye – 59a Milner Road – c.1936.
Mr Rawson – 10 Air Street – c.1936.
S. Rogers – 40 Prestonville Road – c.1936.
Miss Margaret Ryan – 9 Bedford Street – c.1936.

W. *Tullet* – 40 Sussex Terrace – c.1936.
Mrs *Leah Waterman* – 98 North Road – c.1936.
Harry Wilkinson – 83a Edward Street – c.1936.
Alan Wilson – 84 Lewes Road – c.1936.
R.D. Worsley - 41 Brunswick Street East, Hove – early 1970s.
George M. Rich - 39 Tivoli Road – mid-1970s – George's daughter, Jill Prole, runs 'Bookbinders of Lewes'.
F. Vincent Dyer - 79 St. James Street in 1981 – c.1980.

BIBLIOGRAPHY

Allan, G. (2003). *First & Last Editions: England's Second-hand Bookshops.* Brighton/Portland: Alpha Press.

Ashley, M. (2005). *Transformations - the Story of SF Magazines from 1950 to 1970.* Liverpool University Press.

Ballard, J. G. (2008). *Miracles of Life.* 4th Estate.

Beever, D. &. (n.d.). *A Pictorial History of Brighton.* Brighton Borough Council/Breedon Books.

Benjamin, W. (1955). Unpacking My Library: A Talk about Book Collecting (1931). In W. Benjamin, *Illuminations.*

Butler, B. (1975). *The Definitive Tarot.* Rider.

Butler, B. (2001). *Static on Star-filled Winds.* Mike Hughes.

Byng, J. ,. (1788). *A Tour into Sussex.* (manuscript).

Carey, G. S. (1777). *The Tagg, or Brighthelmstone Guide.* Brighton.

Collis, R. &. (2010). *The Encyclopedia of Brighton.*

Cowper Powys, J. (1934). *Autobiography.* The Bodley Head.

Cowper Powys, J. (1938). *The Pleasures of Literature.* Cassell.

Cromwell, T. (1822). *Excursions in the County of Sussex.*

Curwen, H. (1873). *A History of Booksellers: the Old and the New.*

drif. (1991). *drif's guide to the Secondhand & Antiquarian Bookshops in Britain.* drif's field guides.

driff. (1985). *Driff's Guide to All the Secondhand & Antiquarian Bookshops in Britain.* Driffield.

Duncan, A. (2008). *Origins of the Underground.* Salt.

Erredge, J. A. (1862). *The History of Brighthelmston.* Brambletye Books 2005.

Highmore, A. (1782). *A Ramble on the Coast of Sussex.*

Hindley, C. (1871). *The Old Book Collectors Miscellany.* London: Reeves & Turner.

Holleyman, G. (1975). *Catalogue of Books from the Library of Leonard and Virginia Woolf.* Brighton: Holleyman & Treacher - limited edition of 250.

Hollis, M. (2009). "A Dirty and Diseased Mind": the Unicorn Bookshop Trial. Retrieved from www.holli.co.uk/unicorn/text

Johnson, D. (1984). *The Life of Dashiell Hammett.* Chatto & Windus.

Lewis, R. H. (1975). *The Book Browser's Guide: Britain's Secondhand and Antiquarian Bookshops.* David & Charles.

Lewis, R. H. (1978). *Antiquarian Books: An Insider's Account.* Arco.

Low, D. (1973). *With All Faults.* Tehran: The Amate Press.

'M.B'. (1973, April). Anarchist foil bomb plot. *Brighton Voice.*

Newley, P. (1992). In various, *Daring Hearts: Lesbian and Gay Lives of 50s and 60s Brighton.* Brighton: Queenspark Books.

Newley, P. (2006). *The Krays and Bette Davis.* AuthorOnLine.

Norrie, I. (1982). *Mumby's Publishing and Bookselling in the Twentieth Century.* Bell & Hyman.

Noyce, J. (. (1974). *Alternative Brighton.* Brighton: Unicorn.

Ong, M. P. (1996). *Skoob Directory of Secondhand Bookshops in the British Isles - 6th Edition.* London: Skoob.

Orwell, G. (1936). *Bookshop Memories (essay).*

Palmer, T. (1971). *The Trials of OZ.* Blond & Briggs.

Parnell, M. (1968). In R. (. Astbury, *Libraries and the Book Trade - papers delivered at a Symposium held at Liverpool School of Librarianship, May 1967.* London: Clive Bingley.

Philip, A. J. (1927). *The Librarian, International Directory of Booksellers, Publishers, Binders, Paper Makers, Agents etc (Clegg's Successor).*

Puddick, W. a. (1977). *The Underground and Alternative Press in Britain during 1975.* Harvester Press.

'R.D.', (. (1971). *A Directory of Dealers in Secondhand and Antiquarian Books in the British Isles.* London: Sheppard Press.

Rhys, J. (1979). *Smile Please.*

Rolph, C. H. (1969). *Books in the Dock.* Andre Deutsch.

Rota, A. (2000). *International League of Antiquarian Booksellers (ILAB).*

Rota, A. (2006). Defending and Regulating the Trade: 100 Years of the Antiquarian Booksellers Association. In G. (. Mandelbrote, *Out of Print and Into Profit - A History of the*

Rare and Secondhand Book Trade in Britain in the 20th Century. Oak Knoll Press.
Rutherford, J. (1898). *William Moon L.L.D. and his Work for the Blind*. Hodder & Stoughton.
Sala, G. A. (1895). *Brighton As I Have Known It*.
Sinclair, I. (1987). *White Chappell Scarlet Tracings*. Goldmark.
Smith, H. (2002). Brighton Circulating Libraries - an inside view. Quadrat.
Snelling, O. F. (1982). *Rare Books and Rarer People: some personal reminiscences of 'the trade'*. Werner Shaw.
Stephen, C. (2002). Reading and the Circulating Library, Evidence from the Diaries of Charlotte Francis (1798-1870). Quadrat.
Underwood, E. (1978). *Brighton*. London: B.T. Batsford.
unknown. (1769). *The Brighthelmstone Directory &c. &c*. Brighton.
unknown. (1770). *New Brighthelmstone Directory*. Brighton.
unknown. (1899). *Brighton and Hove Almanack*. Brighton.
unknown. (1899). *Brighton and Hove Almanack for 1899*. Brighton.
unknown. (1962). *25 Years of K. J. Bredon's*.
unknown. (1962). *K. J. Bredon's Bookshop: 25 Years*. Brighton: Bredon's.
unknown. (1970, January). *International Times 71*.
unknown. (1972). Bill Butler: Another sort of publisher. *Frendz*.
various. (1979). *Ansible 2/3 (online archive)*. Retrieved from Ansible.
various. (current). *My Brighton & Hove website*.
Wallrich, L. &. (1970). *For Bill Butler*. Wallrich Books.
Woolf, V. (1942). Street Haunting: A London Adventure. In V. Woolf, *The Death of the Moth and Other Essays*.
Wright, S. (1997). *North Laines 'Life Lines' - 76-97 Run with the Runner - Celebrating 21 Years of the North Laine Community Association and the North Laine Runner*. Brighton.

Internet sites.

www.mybrightonandhove.org.uk
- brilliant local history enquiry site.

www.multiverse.org
- Michael Moorcock's welcoming fan site.

www.sheila-markham.com
- interviews with a variety of booksellers.

www.internationaltimes.it
- invaluable archive.

www.regencysociety-jamesgray.com
- excellent historical photographs.

www/bbti/bham.ac.uk
- British book trade index at Birmingham University.

www.thebookseller.com
- indispensable trade news.

www.queensparkbooks.org.uk
- local oral history publishers.

www.brighton-hove-rpml.org.uk/Museums/brightonhistorycentre.

www.ilab.org
- International League of Antiquarian Booksellers

www.fulltable.com
- Chris Mullen's tribute to Holleyman & Treacher.

www.permanentbookshop.com
- at The Permanent Gallery, 20 Bedford Place.

www.davescomicsuk.blogspot.com

Visit the BOOKENDS facebook page for discussions, pictures and more information.

RANDOM MISCELLANEOUS COMPANY
- Acknowledgements

> But here, none too soon, are the second-hand bookshops. Here we find anchorage in these thwarting currents of being; here we balance ourselves after the splendours and miseries of the street...Books are everywhere; and always the same sense of adventure fills us. Second-hand books are wild books, homeless books; they have come together in vast flocks of variegated feather, and have a charm which the domesticated volumes of the library lack. Besides, in this random miscellaneous company we may rub against some complete stranger who will, with luck, turn into the best friend we have in the world...
> The number of books in the world is infinite, and one is forced to glimpse and nod and move on after a moment of talk, a flash of understanding...
>
> - Virginia Woolf
> 'Street Haunting: A London Adventure' 1930
> *The Death of the Moth and Other Essays*, 1942

Immeasurable thanks to -

Alan Sinfield, Adam Trimingham, Pete Deadman, Andrew Duncan, Catriona Reed for unexpected phone calls from California to Devon, Chris Mullen, Colin Page for some fine afternoon wine, Doug Leitch, John Noyce, John Riches (Queenspark Books), Kathy Nichols for the pictures and memories, Alan Nelhams for the same, Kenneth Johnson for an enjoyable drunken afternoon in the pub, Margaret Curson for letting me loose among the stacks, Mark Broad, Karen Eliot,

From BOOKENDS by John Shire (c) 2011

BRIGHTON N W E S

SEVEN DIALS

BRIGHTON STATION

London Road

Trafalgar Street
13 14 15 16
17
1 Gloucester Road
North Laines
21
22

9

10

Dyke Road

Queen's Road

North Road

7
18

Church Street

HOVE ←

Western Road

18 PAVILI
North Street

20

Little Preston St.

Preston Street

19

West Street

Duke St. 4
2
3 Ship St.
South Laines 5

6

King's Road

WEST PIER

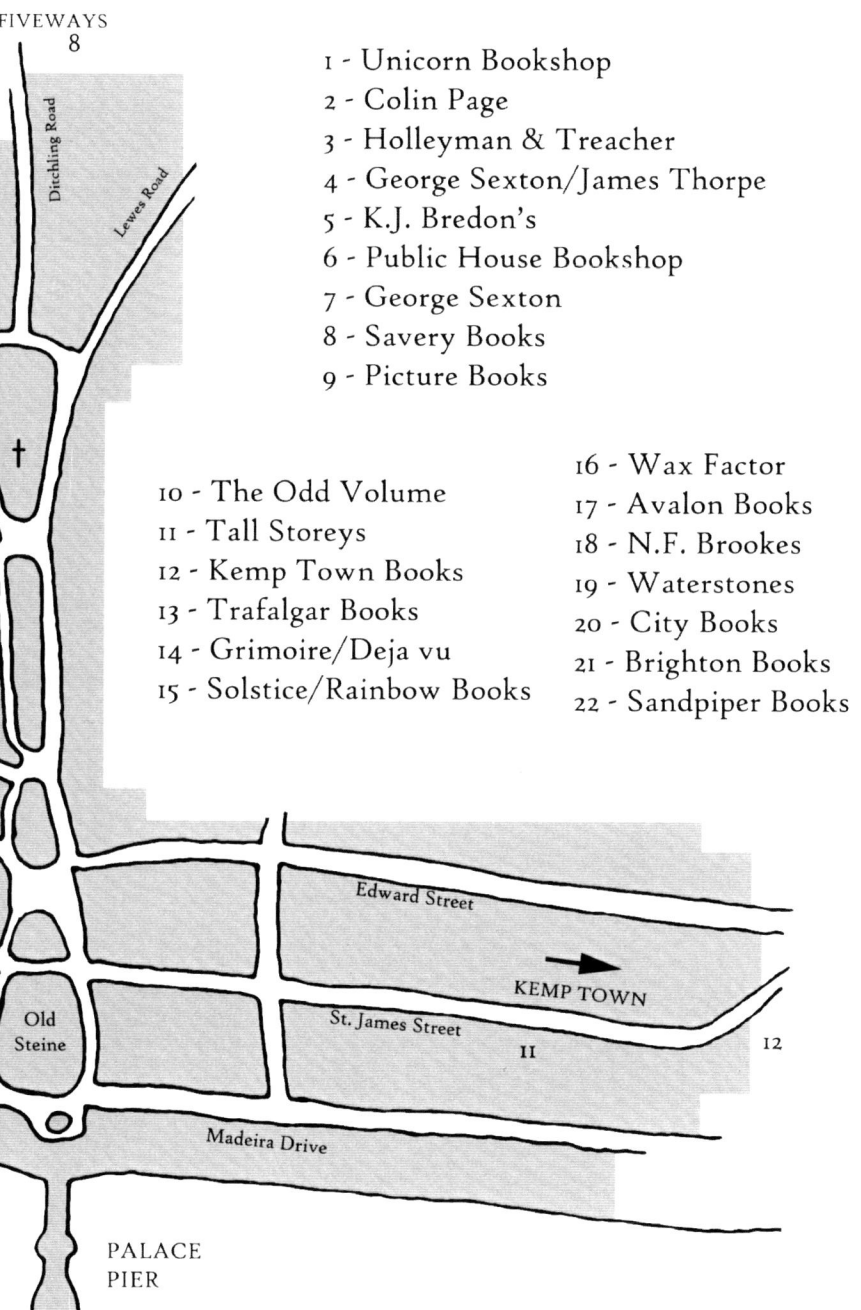

Enoch Soames, Melanie Nowocin, Mike Holliday, Paul Bonnett, Pete Scott for not taking me to Karaoke, Peter Riley, Tom Raworth, Richard Cupidi, Naomi Foyle, Roy Pennington, Sarah Wright, Simon Strong, Spoon-unit, Stefan Szczelkun, Terry Adams, Terry Garoghan, Tony Bennett, David Plumtree, Michael Kadwell, John Loska and all at Colin Page, James & Sheila Keeble, Paul O, Paul Jordan and everyone who assisted at the Brighton History Centre, Lee Harwood, Ananda, Hamilton Wilson, Ben and Meesha at Sandpiper, Anthony Hindson, Steven at Brighton Books, Michael Moorcock and his fine fan site, Andy Grant and all the wonderful people who help to run and contribute to the mybrightonandhove site, Pete Sexton, David Brewer, Ray Russell at Tartarus, Linda Miller, Charlie Booth and Professor John Spiers.

And...

Vicky, Ella and Tanya for putting up with this nonsense ("It's been a lifetime!" said Ella. She's ten.), Mike and Helen in whose company I have captured many a strange city (Beware the Fall of Evil Empires!), Cyril for many things, Mum for everything, Michael, without whose IT support none of this would have been possible, Richard and Esther, Simon, Kaz and the whole zavvi/Virgin crew, Rod, Andy, Leon, Vincent, Gideon and Hayley.

And to everyone who helped along the way.

INDEX

A

Alternative Brighton	52, 61
Argus, Evening	30, 33, 71
Arkham House	8
Atlantis (London)	102
Attila	52, 76
Avalon Books	36, 79, 100, **101**, 128

B

Ball, Adam/Grimoire	7, 79, **99**, 138
Ballard, J. G.	40, 47, 51
Banks, Brian/Déja Vu	97, 101
Bassam, Steve	72, 86
Beal's	74, **88**
Benjamin, Walter	1
Bennett, Tony	54-56, 66
Better Books (London)	39, 43, 51, 53, 102
Bioscope Books	64-65, 67, 74, 97, 116
Blackwells	33
Bloomfield, Leonard L.	27
Bonnett, Paul	63, 68, 78, 136
Book Collecting & Library Monthly	121
Book Nook	138
Booth Museum	89, 106
Borders	33, 66, 130, 139
Body Shop	64
Bowden, Andrew	78
Bredon's (K.J.)/Sussex Stationers	74, **88**, 113, 129, 140
Brewer, David	83
Briggs, Raymond	67
Brighton Books (1972)	61, 74
Brighton Books (current)	120, 128, 132
Brighton Combination	71
Brighton Festival	77
Brighton Head & Freak Mag	71

Brighton Museum	92, 114
Brighton Pavilion	8, 11
Brighton Voice	72, 75-76, 78-79, 86-87
Brimstone's	7, 111, 119, 132
Brookes, Noel F.	1, 7, 67, 74, 85, **105**, 119, 140
Burney, Fanny	11, 14
Burroughs, William	39, 47, 48, 59, 119
Butler, Bill	27, 30, **35**, 61, 69, 70, 98, 102, 121, 137
Butler, Neil	86
Byng, John (5th Viscount Torrington)	11

C

Camilla's (Francombe)	83-84
Carr-Gomm, Philip	98
Catalogues	26
Children of Albion (Michael Horowitz ed.)	46
Circulating Libraries	9-17, 97
City Books	32, 132
City Lights (USA)	60, 66, 77
Cobbing, Bob	46, 53, 77
Combridge's	74, **88**, 112, 128, 137
Compendium (London)	60, 62, 102
Courthouse Steps	7, 136
Cowley Club	60
Cromwell, Thomas	15
Crowley, Aleister	31, 49, 54, 89, 97, 102
Cunliffe, Professor Barry	114
Cupidi, Richard	54, **70**, 121, 136

D

Dark They Were & Golden-Eyed (London)	67
David's (Paine)	89, 129, 132, 138
Dean, Neal	73
Dedalus Press	131
Deptford Albany Theatre	71
Disch, Thomas M.	51
Dodds, John	83

Dragon's Gate	60, 104
Driffield	69, 83-84, 97, 101, 106, 127-129, 136
Duke, Jim	71
Duke Street	26, 30, 31, 121, 123, 132
Dwyer, Simon	103
Dyke Road	29, 32, 83

E

ECM (record label)	76
Edwards, Richard H. Quinton	32, 36, 138
English Language Bookshop	138

F

Folthorp, Robert (Royal Library & Guide)	16, 41
For Bill Butler	46
Fowler, W. F.	31
Friend, D. B.	23, 26
Frit Freight	49-50

G

Ginsberg, Allen	39, 42, 46, 48, 67, 77
Goldman, Arnold	44, 45
Grant, William	16-17
Graphic Novel Shop	129, 138
Greene, Graham	44, 49, 127
Greer, Germaine	36

H

Hanningtons	22, 112
Harvester Press	137
Harwood, Lee	41, 42, 48, 53, 70, 77, 121
Highmore, Anthony	14
Hindley, Charles	19, 21
Hindson, Anthony	61, 62
Holleyman, George	84, **112**, 123, 138
Holleyman & Treacher	7, 31, 74, **112**, 136
Howes Bookshop (Hastings)	116, 137-139

Hughes, Michael   39, 54, 58, 98
Hutchinson, Ben   56, 74, 97, **120**, 137

I
Infinity Foods   52, 68, 72
International Times (IT)   38, 39, 71
Invisible Books (Snooper's Paradise)   128
Ipads   130

J
Johnson, Kenneth (Rayner)   **100**
Josef K Bookshop   138
Jubilee Library   12, 28

K
Kadwell, Michael   117, 136
Kemp Town Bookshop   7, 32, 127, 128, 132
Kieffer, John   77
Knockabout Comics   56
Kilgariff, Raymond   116

L
Lane, Kenny   74, 89
Latest Homes   78, 86
Lepper, David   72
Lewes   9, 111, 123
Loska, John   110-111, 119, **120**
Lovecraft, H.P.   8
Low, David   30, 49, 129
Lucas, Edward Verrall   22, 140

M
MacBeth, George   44, 46
Machen, Arthur   106, 109
Masons   26-27, 30, 97, 138
McCarthy, Pete   86
Mears, Ray   80

Metcalfe-Morton, John	26-27, 117
Miller, Tony	**83**, 136
Moon, William	24
Moorcock, Michael	40, 47, 51, 54, 57
Moore, Alan	56
Morley, Edward/Edwin Gaius	29-30, 138
Mortimer, John, QC	37, 43
Moseley, Ruth and Richard	137
Mottram, Eric	44, 46, 48, 77, 79

N

National Front	68, 75, 78-79
Nelhams, Alan	92
Net Book Agreement (NBA)	33, 80, 119, 129
New Worlds	47, 51
Newley, Patrick	50
North, James Sharpe	115
Nuttall, Jeff	46, 48, 63

O

Oak, Ash & Thorn Press	137
Occult	27, 49, 60, **96**
Odd Volume	36, 80, **82**, 106
Ogden, C. K.	98
Old Bookhouse	27
Olivier, Laurence	84, 93
Open Café	72
Open Door	63
Orwell, George	3, 26, 132
Out!	36
OZ	36-39, 42, 44, 53

P

Page, Colin	7, 57, 111, 119, **120**, 132
Parnell, Martin	42, 60, 93
Permanent Bookshop & Gallery	138
Picture Books	82

Plumtree, David	117, 136
Powys, John Cowper	iii, 3-5, 18-21, 31, 38, 43, 100, 110, 134
Public House Bookshop	36, 52, 67, **70**, 118, 138
Practical Books	33, 74
Print-on-demand (POD)	130
Punter	86-87

Q

Quadrant	74, 107
Queen's Road	1, 31, 39, 40, **105**
Quinto's	7

R

Rainbow Books	96, 120, 132
Rapid Eye	103
Rare Books & Special Collection (Jubilee Library)	28, 82, 139
Read All About It	33, 118
Reed, Chris/Caitriona	61-63
Reeve, Philip	34
Ripper, Herbert J.	44
Robinson's Bookshop	74, 90
Rossmore Express Books	40
Rota, Anthony	29, 113
Russell, Dr Richard	9, 13

S

Sandilands Family	24
Sandpiper Books	106, 132, 140
Savery Books	120, 132
Scott, Pete	57, 108, 111
Seacon (SF Convention)	67
Sexton, George	7, 29-30, 74, 122, 137-138
Ship Street	30, 137
Sinclair, Iain	77, 83, 130
Sinfield, Alan	35
'Smallest Theatre in the World'	73
Smith, Bill	78, 85-86

Smith, Clark Ashton	8
Smith, Ken	122
Smith, Raymond	92-93
Smith, W.J. ('Smith's Cuttings')	18, 121
Snake River Press	137
Solstice	36, **59**, 74, 79, 96, 98
Sotheby's	122
Spinrad, Norman	47
Sprague, Sean	62
Studio Bookshop	7, 120, 128, 132
Summers, Montague	98
Supermarkets	33
Survival Scrapbooks	51-52, 54, 65
Sussex University	45, 68, 72, 80, 83, 128
Symposium	36, **59**, 79, 98
Szelkun, Stefan	48, 52

T

Tall Storeys	7, **82**, 119, 139
Tartarus Press	109
Tauchnitz Editions	121
Theatre Bookshop	32, 65, 74
Thorpe, James	29, 137
Townley	32
Trafalgar Bookshop	7, 64, 98, 119
Trafalgar Street	7, 30, 31, 63-65, 69, 78, **96**, 121, 132
Traylen, Charles	138
Treacher's, H. & C.	22, 23, 28, 112
Two-Way Books	74, 128, 132

U

Unicorn Bookshop	27, 30, **35**, 61, 70, 74, 88, 101, 107, 129, 138
Upton, John	39, 72, 77

V

Valiente, Doreen	49
Virgin Records	63, 65, 131

Vortex	67, 138
W	
W. H. Smith	47, 59, 139
Walton, Catherine	100
Ward, Frederick J.	90-91
Waterstone's	5, 36, 130, 131, 139
Watkins Bookshop (London)	103
Wax Factor	99, 102, 116, 127, 132
Wellesbourne	10, 31
White, Graham	119
Whole Earth Catalog	65
Woolf, Virginia	115, 117

And now the book
Ends.